# At ✱ Issue

# How Does Religion Influence Politics?

James D. Torr, *Book Editor*

Bonnie Szumski, *Publisher*
Helen Cothran, *Managing Editor*

**GREENHAVEN PRESS**
*An imprint of Thomson Gale, a part of The Thomson Corporation*

**THOMSON**
━━━━━✱━━━━━ ™
**GALE**

Detroit • New York • San Francisco • San Diego • New Haven, Conn.
Waterville, Maine • London • Munich

*For more information, contact*
Greenhaven Press
27500 Drake Rd.
Farmington Hills, MI 48331-3535
Or you can visit our Internet site at http://www.gale.com

Greenhaven Press anthologies primarily consist of previously published material taken from a variety of sources, including periodicals, books, scholarly journals, newspapers, government documents, and position papers from private and public organizations. These original sources are often edited for length and to ensure their accessibility for a young adult audience. The anthology editors also change the original titles of these works in order to clearly present the main thesis of each viewpoint and to explicitly indicate the opinion presented in the viewpoint. These alterations are made in consideration of both the reading and comprehension levels of a young adult audience. Every effort is made to ensure that Greenhaven Press accurately reflects the original intent of the authors included in this anthology.

Cover credit: © Comstock/PhotoDisc/U.S. Senate Photo Studio

| LIBRARY OF CONGRESS CATALOGING-IN-PUBLICATION DATA |
| --- |
| How does religion influence politics? / Torr, James D., book editor. |
|    p. cm. — (At issue) |
| Includes bibliographical references and index. |
| ISBN 0-7377-3425-6 (lib. : alk. paper) — ISBN 0-7377-3426-4 (pbk. : alk. paper) |
|    1. Christianity and politics—United States. 2. Religion and politics. |
| 3. Christianity—Influence. 4. Religions—Influence. I. Torr, James D., 1974– |
| II. At issue (San Diego, Calif.) |
| BR115.P7H595 2006 |
| 322'.1'0973—dc22                                           2005052568 |

Printed in the United States of America

# Contents

# Introduction

One of the biggest stories to emerge from the 2004 presidential election revolved around the concept of the "values vote." In a CNN poll of those who had just voted, one-fifth said that "moral values" was the most important issue for them in choosing a candidate—more important than terrorism, Iraq (with which the United States was engaged in war), or the economy—and 80 percent of these "values voters" voted for George W. Bush. Bush captured about 51 percent of the popular vote, compared to Democratic candidate John Kerry's 48.5 percent, leading many political analysts to suggest that the Democrats' failure to capture more of the values vote may have cost them the election.

Polling data had revealed this "values gap" months before the election. Moreover, the data suggested that the "values gap" was largely a "religion gap," since religion was the key factor that influenced values voters. In October 2004, the Pew Research Center for the People and the Press found that 63 percent of Americans who attend religious services more than once a week planned to vote Republican, while 62 percent of voters who seldom or never attend services said they would vote Democratic. Similarly, a June 2004 *Time* poll found that 59 percent of voters who consider themselves "very religious" supported Bush, while 69 percent of those who considered themselves "not religious" supported Kerry. Some analysts, such as Trinity College religion professor Mark Silk, maintain that the religion gap is wider than ever: "Never before in American history have churches been tied so directly to one political party."

Religious voters likely support Bush because they identify with Bush's religiosity. As *Washington Post* staff writer Alan Cooperman explains,

> George W. Bush is among the most openly religious presidents in U.S. history. A daily Bible reader, he often talks about how Jesus changed his heart. He has spoken, publicly and privately, of hearing God's call to run for the presidency and of praying for God's help since he came into office.

Many conservative religious voters also support Bush because he has the same views as they do on the issues most important to them. For example, Bush has opposed government funding for embryonic stem-cell research. (Pro-life religious conservatives have lobbied against such research because it involves the destruction of human embryos.) Bush also supported a faith-based initiative under which religious organizations that provide community services may receive government funding. Bush's stance on these issues may be a reflection of his personal beliefs, but it may also be part of the Republican party's very effective political strategy of catering to religious voters.

In contrast, political analysts agree that the Democrats have had less success applying religious doctrines to their political positions. In his 2004 campaign, John Kerry did try to appeal to religious voters. "Let me say it plainly," he announced in his acceptance speech at the September 2004 Democratic Convention, "in this campaign, we welcome people of faith." However, in the media Kerry's emphasis on his Catholic faith was often treated with skepticism, since he opposed the church on issues such as abortion and same-sex marriage. The controversy was exacerbated when, during the 2004 campaign, some Catholic leaders suggested that churches should refuse communion to pro-choice politicians. This served to focus attention on Kerry's stance on abortion rather than on his message of inclusiveness. The overall effect was that Kerry's public religious expressions did not resonate with voters in the same way that Bush's did.

Another reason that Democrats have failed to close the religion gap is that they have traditionally been the defenders of separation of church and state. As *Nation* journalist Eyal Press writes, "Democrats have traditionally opposed efforts by social conservatives to impose their religious beliefs on other Americans, a stance that often leaves them open to attacks as 'antireligious.'" Because of this, many political analysts have argued that the party needs to emphasize that political candidates can be religious and yet support the separation of religion from government.

Finally, many liberals are *not* very religious and do not believe that religion has a place in politics. Liberals who hold these views have sometimes weakened Democrats' attempts to court religious voters. For example, in the 2000 presidential election, Democrat Joe Lieberman, Al Gore's running mate, was criticized by some liberal groups for speaking about how his Jewish faith informed his political beliefs. Most notably, the Jewish Anti-

Defamation League objected that mixing religious expression and political discourse was "contrary to the American ideal." The distaste that some liberal voters have for mixing religion and politics may discourage Democratic candidates from being more open about their faith.

The majority of Americans, both liberal and conservative, believe that religion and politics need not be separate. In a nationally representative November 2003 Zogby's poll, only 36 percent of Americans said that religion should "not at all" play a role in public policy. Moreover, 90 percent reported that religion plays a significant role in their lives, and 56 percent said that their religious beliefs play some role in how they vote.

The way in which religion influences politics is the subject of endless debate among pollsters and political analysts. While opinions vary on how much a role religion *should* play in politics, there is no question that it plays a significant one. As *Time* journalist Nancy Gibbs puts it, "Church and state may be separate, but faith and politics are not."

# 1

# Religion Plays an Important Role in Politics

## Suzanne Fields

*Suzanne Fields is a columnist for the* Washington Times.

Some political pundits are uncomfortable with politicians who speak openly about their religious beliefs. In particular, critics of George W. Bush have charged that the president's faith determines his policy decisions. However, a person's faith will always influence his or her decisions and can provide helpful guidance in solving problems. A political candidate's public religious expressions are grounds for criticism only when they smack of self-righteousness or are used to justify violence and deception. America's leaders should not be disparaged simply for speaking about their faith.

It's a lot easier to talk about sex and money at a Washington dinner party than about religion and spiritual matters. Religion popped into a discussion of Renaissance art at such a dinner party the other night in Washington. I remarked, innocently I thought, that certain paintings, such as Masaccio's *Expulsion of Adam and Eve from Paradise* and Raphael's *Madonna and Child*, as well as Michelangelo's sculpture of the *Pieta*, inspired a profound spiritual reflection.

Several guests more accustomed to talking politics than religion seemed shocked to be dining with such a zealot, and argued that many Quattrocento [fifteenth-century] artists who

Suzanne Fields, "One Noisy Nation, Under God; Faith's Important Role in Politics," *Washington Times*, June 21, 2004, p. A19. Copyright © 2004 by the *Washington Times*. All rights reserved. Distributed by Valeo IP.

created gorgeous "religious" works merely used religious themes as vehicles for sensual color and line because that's where the money was—in churches and rich papist patrons.

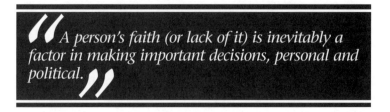

*A person's faith (or lack of it) is inevitably a factor in making important decisions, personal and political.*

The subject was quickly changed to the safer one of presidential politics, but the next day I received a call from one of the guests who wanted to continue the conversation on the topic of "spiritual reflection." She remarked, sadly, that many Americans with sophistication and education could only talk about religion in "intellectual" terms.

## Faith and Character

Pundits mocked [President] George W. Bush when, during the 2000 campaign, he told an interviewer that Jesus Christ was the most influential philosopher in his life, though this was not so remarkable to anyone actually conversant with our nation's history. *Time* magazine notes in its [June 21, 2004] cover story, "Faith, God and the Oval Office," that Thomas Jefferson said the same thing 200 years ago. Spirituality and adherence to certain religions (like "sophistication" and "education") can be faked by artists, politicians and the rest of us for all kinds of reasons, but public religious expression seems to make those without faith particularly uncomfortable.

As this [2004] election season unfolds, it behooves all of us to be particularly judicious and discriminating in the ways we interpret what a person says about his faith. Those who criticize George W.'s religious talk fear that his faith determines policy. But a person's faith (or lack of it) is inevitably a factor in making important decisions, personal and political. Stem-cell research and abortion are issues that atheists as well as the faithful can question because profound and complex issues determine how we value life. Not even a saint has all the answers to every question.

A young Catholic man once told me that he sought out a priest to tell him how to solve a problem that he had to solve for himself. The priest told him, "I know two things for sure," he said. "I know there is a God and I know that I'm not Him." Religion doesn't determine who we are; it guides us through the faltering steps of life. An atheist, like a believer, can have a deep ethical core to guide him in determining what's right and wrong.

When religion is used to justify violence and deception, abuse and exploitation, "faith" becomes a weapon of mass destruction. The president is correct when he says that terrorists may "couch their language in religious terms, but that doesn't make them religious people."

Americans are among the most religious people in the world—the nation was founded by men who sought a place to worship freely—and ours is among the most tolerant nations in the world. But the nation's roots are Judeo-Christian, and it's Christianity that most often carries the national ideals, first expressed in the Declaration of Independence, into the public square.

## Freedom for Religion

This confuses some people who ought to know better. "This is rapidly becoming the most religiously infused political campaign in modern history," says Barry Lynn, executive director of Americans United for Separation of Church and State. Mr. Lynn never seems to hear a public religious expression that doesn't ruin his day. This observation is absurd. The doctrine of separation of church and state has never meant separation of a candidate from his religion, or a society from its spiritual roots. It was meant to be freedom for religion.

[French author] Alexis de Tocqueville understood this when he argued that religious mores mitigate and socialize self-interest and that only in America was "the spirit of religion and the spirit of freedom" successfully combined, allowing a vital religious life to support public cooperation for the common good.

A candidate's religious references in a political campaign are fair game for debate, and when piety morphs into self-righteousness we should note it. But when we look at a man's religion we must be careful to see the whole man, how he orders his life and not just what he says he believes. We live in dangerous times, and spiritual reflection, whether driven by preacher, painter or politician, should be welcomed. That's what it means to live in "one nation under God."

# 2

# Religion Plays Too Large a Role in Politics

## Cathy Young

*Cathy Young is a columnist for the* Boston Globe *and a contributing editor of* Reason *magazine.*

Both Democrats and Republicans are guilty of mixing religion and politics. Religion was a major issue in the 2004 presidential election, and some political analysts argued that the campaigns of Democratic candidates John Kerry and Howard Dean suffered not because of their political views, but because the two men were viewed as being less religious than Republican nominee George W. Bush. Indeed, polls indicate that 70 percent of Americans want their presidential candidate to be religious. However, approximately one-third of Americans also say that religion is not very important in their lives. In order to be fair to this nonreligious minority, and to secular candidates, religion should play a lesser role in politics.

When John F. Kennedy ran for President in 1960, his Roman Catholic faith was widely viewed as a stumbling block to his campaign. Many voters feared that Catholic politicians would look to the Vatican for guidance, putting their loyalty to the Church above their obligations to the American people.

Kennedy responded by reiterating his absolute commitment to the separation of church and state. In a September 1960 address to the Greater Houston Ministerial Association, he declared his belief in "an America where . . . no Catholic prelate would tell the president [should he be Catholic] how to act."

Fast-forward 44 years to the presidential campaign of another Catholic Democrat from Massachusetts, Senator John Kerry. This time around, the charge is that he is *insufficiently* loyal to the Catholic Church.

In June 2004, the Los Angeles–based Catholic lawyer Mark Balestrieri filed heresy charges against Kerry with the Boston Archdiocese, asking that he be excommunicated because of his support for legal abortion. Around the same time, Pope John Paul II's doctrinal adviser, Cardinal Ratzinger, sent a memo to the U.S. Conference of Catholic Bishops stating that politicians who support abortion rights should be denied communion. Four American bishops already had said they would deny Kerry communion.

> *'One day, a truly secular candidate might be able to run for president without suffering at the polls. But that day won't be soon.'*

Some commentators—including several conservatives, such as the *Weekly Standard*'s Terry Eastland—noted that such tactics could backfire. But the controversy was generally seen as a liability and an embarrassment for Kerry. In his speech accepting the Democratic nomination at his party's convention in July [2004], Kerry asserted that he did not wear his faith on his sleeve, yet much of his speech was crafted in religious terms.

Religion in politics has come a long way since 1960.

## Faith as a Litmus Test for the Presidency

Kerry is not the first Democratic candidate to have a religion problem this campaign. The former front-runner, Howard Dean, was labeled too secular to be electable. A January 2004 cover story by Franklin Foer in the *New Republic* declared that Dean would have trouble shedding the "liberal" image—less because of his politics than because he was "one of the most secular candidates to run for president in modern history." (Dean, an Episcopalian turned Congregationalist, had openly said that he didn't go to church often and that religion didn't inform his public policy views.)

Other publications picked up on this theme. In a particularly bizarre moment, an interview with Dean by *Newsweek's* Howard Fineman abruptly turned from various policy issues to the question, "Do you see Jesus Christ as the son of God and believe in him as the route to salvation and eternal life?"

It's hard to tell whether the meteoric fall of Dean's candidacy had anything to do with his perceived secularism—or, for that matter, with his clumsy attempt to reinvent himself as a man of faith. Nonetheless, few would disagree with Foer's statement, "One day, a truly secular candidate might be able to run for president without suffering at the polls. But that day won't be soon."

Article VI of the U.S. Constitution explicitly states that "no religious test shall ever be required as a qualification to any office or public trust." But formal tests are one thing, voter preferences another; no one can keep the people from imposing a religious litmus test on candidates. Today that litmus test is not membership in a particular religion but religiosity in general—though it's hard to tell how the public would react to a Muslim or a Hindu candidate. In a 2000 Pew Research Center poll, 70 percent of Americans said that they wanted a presidential candidate to be religious.

The prominence of religion in the Bush White House makes secularist liberals profoundly nervous. Four of the six blurbs on the back of Susan Jacoby's *Freethinkers: A History of American Secularism*, published in May 2004, refer directly or indirectly to the Bush presidency—what Arthur Schlesinger Jr. called, in his blurb, "the tide of religiosity engulfing a once secular republic."

The real picture, as usual, is more complex. Indeed, Jacoby's fascinating if flawed history demonstrates that religiosity and secularism have always been competing strains in American public life. In a cyclical pattern, relatively secular periods have been followed by religious upsurges.

## Religiosity on the Left

There is no question that religion and politics are entangled today in ways that would have been unthinkable in 1960. But blaming this solely on the right is disingenuous. Jimmy Carter was the first modern president to wear his faith on his sleeve. In 2000 [Democratic presidential candidate] Al Gore claimed that "What would Jesus do?" was his guide to making policy, while his running mate, Joe Lieberman, talked of renewing "the dedication of our nation and ourselves to God and God's purpose."

Critics of Christian conservatives are often blind to it, but religion and politics mix freely on the left as well as the right, from Quaker peace activism to the role black churches play in mobilizing the African-American vote. Last April [2003], in a review of *The Jesus Factor*, a PBS program about the role of Bush's evangelical faith in his presidency, *Salon* critic Charles Taylor stated with startlingly unselfconscious candor that the scary thing about Bush was not that he injected his faith into politics, but that he was using it to promote a right-wing rather than left-wing agenda—in Taylor's words, to serve narrow constituencies rather than a "legitimate civil interest" such as raising taxes on the rich.

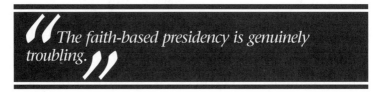

*The faith-based presidency is genuinely troubling.*

Given the liberal intelligentsia's high tolerance for the use of traditional religion in progressive causes, it's not surprising that hardly anyone questions the political influence of Earth-worshipping environmentalism, which novelist Michael Crichton has called "the religion of choice for urban atheists." This environmentalist "spirituality" pervades Gore's 1992 book *Earth in the Balance.*

There is some truth to the conservative claim that liberal hand wringing about the intrusion of faith into politics often smacks of politically correct bigotry. The war in Iraq and the War on Terror were widely portrayed as a part of Bush's religiously inspired crusade against "evildoers." Many Bush critics, from British political commentator Rupert Cornwell in the *Independent* to Jim Wallis of the liberal evangelical magazine *Sojourners*, have even decried his use of the word *evil*, in reference to people who crash airplanes into buildings, as evidence of religious fanaticism.

## The Anti-Secularist Bias

Yet the faith-based presidency is genuinely troubling. This is not only because of the public policies justified by invoking God's name. No less important is the symbolic message that one must be religious in order to be a part of the body politic—in order, perhaps, to be a "real" American. It's a message that goes hand in hand with a good deal of secularist bashing and particularly atheist bashing: In some of the Republican attacks on Democratic financier George Soros, *atheist* was used as a term of opprobrium.

The public's views on this subject are more complex than the champions of religion in the public square often make them out to be. For instance, a recent *Time* poll found likely voters evenly divided on the question of whether the president should allow his personal faith to be his guide in making political decisions. The vast majority of Americans consider themselves religious, but about a third do not consider religion very important in their lives and attend religious services once a month or less. That's a pretty large segment of the population to reduce to the status of political pariahs.

The idea that politicians should keep their religious faith private may seem outrageously intolerant. But is it not equally outrageous that, on today's political scene, a secularist figure cannot express his views honestly without committing career suicide? Unlikely though it is to happen, a moratorium on God talk might level the playing field.

# 3

# Religious Groups Should Be Wary of Becoming Too Involved in Politics

## A. James Reichley

*A. James Reichley is a senior fellow at the Public Policy Institute at Georgetown University and the author of* Faith in Politics, *from which the following viewpoint is excerpted.*

Historically, churches have been very influential in shaping the government's stance on issues such as prohibition, civil rights, women's suffrage, and the abolition of slavery. Churches can be particularly helpful in helping Americans make sense of ethical issues such as abortion and stem-cell research. However, churches should be careful about how actively they become involved in the political process. If they become too involved in routine politics, they risk being viewed as just another special interest group, and thus lose their moral credibility.

"Why don't the churches just shut up?" Peter Berger [a professor of sociology and theology at Boston University] asked, expressing perhaps temporary exasperation over the flurry of social and political pronouncements that have issued in recent times from religious leaders and groups. Many, both within and outside the faith communities, agree that some religious bodies have been drawn too deeply into secular politics. But the memory of events in Germany during the 1920s and 1930s sets an outer limit to the degree of political noninvolvement that most religious people now feel is morally acceptable for churches or other religious groups.

Despite a few honorable exceptions, most German churches and church leaders made little effort to oppose, and some even actively supported, the rise to power and brutal conduct of Adolf Hitler and the Nazi party. The Lutheran doctrine of the "two kingdoms" proved simply inadequate to deal with a situation in which the civil power came to be dominated by a monster like Hitler. German Catholics or Calvinists, who lacked even the excuse of doctrinal inhibition, did little better in showing resistance to the Nazis.

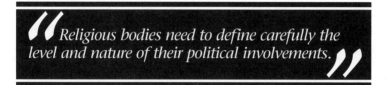

*Religious bodies need to define carefully the level and nature of their political involvements.*

There is now a consensus in most faiths that such noninvolvement must never be permitted to happen again: that faith must oppose extreme social evil even at the risk of its own worldly survival. Whatever differences exist over its interpretation (and they are many), the principle is firmly established: organized religion is morally bound to do what it can to resist political despotism or terror.

Beyond this point of consensus, opinions differ widely on the appropriate role for religion in secular politics. Some religious leaders hold that faith should concern itself almost solely with salvation of individual souls, and therefore regard practically all political involvement by religion beyond resistance to tyranny as irrelevant distraction. Others favor intense participation by the churches in all kinds of economic, social, and foreign policy issues, or even formation of a religious political party, perhaps modeled on the Christian Democratic parties in Europe or the religious parties in Israel.

The approaches taken by particular churches to political action are conditioned by their histories and by the current social needs and interests of their members. Most Jewish groups are naturally dedicated to support for Israel. The traditional role of African American churches as centers of social organization leads them to act as political advocates for black interests. Catholic concern that education be oriented toward religion produces a special outlook on church-state relations—now increasingly shared by evangelical Christians and Orthodox Jews operating their own schools. Some Catholics are tugged in different directions by the issues of abortion and social welfare. Evangelical Protestants are particularly aroused by the growing secularization of American society. Mainline Protestants are influenced by the precedents of church participation in the struggles for abolition, Prohibition, and women's suffrage. "Peace" churches like the Quakers and the Mennonites campaign for arms reduction. Mormons join evangelical Protestants and some Catholics and mainline Protestants in support for traditional moral values.

Some differences among religious groups in their approaches to politics will no doubt continue into the indefinite future. To perform both their social and their more purely religious functions effectively, however, religious bodies need to define carefully the level and nature of their political involvements. This work of definition requires consideration of several conceptual and strategic questions.

## When Religious Bodies Weigh in, Political Stakes Escalate

*Should religious bodies take stands on issues that are socially divisive?* Some social issues that involve major moral questions, like abortion, stem cell research, and oppostion to economic globalization, are profoundly divisive within the larger society. When religious bodies become politically active on these issues, they inevitably, if they are at all influential, push higher the emotional heat in what may already be an explosive social environment, and may make pragmatic compromise more difficult.

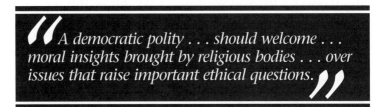

*A democratic polity . . . should welcome . . . moral insights brought by religious bodies . . . over issues that raise important ethical questions.*

Church leaders often speak of their responsibility to be socially prophetic in the manner of the prophets of ancient Israel. This formulation exaggerates the relevance of a precedent drawn from a very different social system. The Hebrew prophets operated in a nondemocratic polity that had no institutional equivalent of an elected opposition or a free press. Under a democratic system, primarily political institutions are normally available to represent most of the socially aggrieved. Nevertheless, the churches can hardly avoid taking stands on issues that, according to the principles of their creeds, involve fundamental moral issues. This has been true for mainline Protestants, Catholics, and Jews on civil rights, for many church groups on the nuclear arms issue, and for Catholics and evangelical Protestants on abortion.

The larger society must hope that the churches and other religious groups will express their positions on issues of this kind with due regard for the rights of citizens who do not share their convictions and for the continued viability of democratic processes. But a democratic polity cannot restrict, and in fact should welcome, as a counterweight to necessary but potentially demoralizing pragmatism, moral insights brought by religious bodies to debates over issues that raise important ethical questions.

On some issues churches have at times felt obliged to recommend, or at least to countenance, actual violation of civil law as a means of expressing protest against prevailing government policies. Examples include the abolitionists of the 1850s, the suffragettes of the early decades of the twentieth century, and the civil rights activists and antiwar protesters of the 1960s. Currently, some religious groups threaten civil disobedience to halt abortion, and others promote protests against economic globalization. Such actions obviously escalate the legal and political stakes—as the protesters intend. They can, however, be honored by a system of government through law so long as they stop short of violence and so long as the protesters are prepared to accept prescribed civil or criminal penalties for their acts. Protesters breaking a civil law to make a political point are within a tradition that pluralist democracy under normal circumstances can accept and sometimes learn from. But protesters who resort to violence or expect to escape legally prescribed punishments are placing themselves in defiance to the entire system of government through law that is among democracy's essential supports. . . .

## Religious Bodies as Moral Authorities

*Is every political issue a moral issue?* Practically every decision made by government, even if it involves no more than changing the physical location of a government office, touches moral concerns at some point. The extent of these moral dimensions, however, varies greatly. Some issues, such as civil rights or nuclear war or abortion, are fundamentally, though almost never exclusively, moral in nature. At the other extreme are issues, like administrative reform or choice of government contractors, that normally turn on questions that are primarily technical or pragmatic. In between lies a wide range of issues that raise significant moral questions but on which persons operating on similar moral assumptions may come down on different sides because of differing technical or empirical judgments.

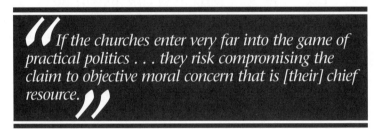

*If the churches enter very far into the game of practical politics . . . they risk compromising the claim to objective moral concern that is [their] chief resource.*

Some religious bodies may reasonably and responsibly decide to take stands on public issues in this middle range when the moral component is strong, such as abuse or exploitation of children, persistent poverty, defense of families, help for the physically or mentally disabled, suppression of pornography, regulation of tobacco and alcohol, protection of the natural environment, and limitation of gun use. On other issues, religious bodies may play useful roles as fact gatherers, sponsors of public forums, or mediators. To perform such roles effectively, religious bodies need to cultivate reputations for objectivity and open-mindedness. These qualities are not likely to be associated with participation by churches or other religious bodies as partisan combatants or propagandists for the political left of right.

## The Moral Taint of Politics

*Should religious bodies operate in politics like ordinary interest groups?* Most economic, social, and ideological interest groups pursue their political objectives in part through pragmatic exchanges of favors with public officeholders and with other interest groups—in short, through political logrolling. When religious bodies or coalitions become involved in politics, they are naturally tempted to play by standard political rules. Some conventional interest-group techniques, such as publishing tabulations of how legislators have voted on selected issues, can probably be adopted by religious groups without undue danger to their moral standing. But if the churches enter very far into the game of practical politics as it is usually played, they risk compromising the claim to objective moral concern that is the chief resource most of them bring to the political table.

A mainline leader said off the record, for example, that he believed increasing the earned income tax credit was a more effective means than increasing the minimum wage to help low-income earners, but that he supported raising the minimum wage to maintain ties with the labor unions—a normal tactic for an ordinary interest group but questionable from a group claiming to represent moral authority.

When religious groups take a stand on political or economic issues, that position should be perceived to represent independent moral judgment, not obligation to a network of allied interest groups. Otherwise religious bodies or coalitions will soon come to be regarded as just one more interest group without any legitimate claim on moral conscience.

*Should religious groups become directly involved in political campaigns?* Federal tax laws prohibit churches that enjoy tax exemptions from endorsing or actively supporting candidates for public office. Many black churches, and more recently some conservative fundamentalist preachers, have operated on the edge of this prohibition. Some church leaders, both liberal and conservative, argue that tax laws should be changed so that churches in the United States can participate directly in politics, as their counterparts do in many European countries.

On occasion, churches may feel obliged to give tacit support to particular candidates or parties as the only practical means for advancing their moral objectives. But as a rule, the more deeply churches become involved in the electoral side of politics, the greater the dangers of undermining their primary spiritual and moral functions and of unleashing tendencies that threaten the political system's capacity for achieving practical compromise.

## Religion and the Public Good

From the standpoint of the public good, the most important service that religious bodies offer to secular life in a free society is to nurture moral values that help humanize capitalism and give direction to democracy. Up to a point, participation by churches and other religious bodies in the formation of public policy, particularly on issues with clear moral content, probably strengthens their ability to perform this nurturing function. But if religious bodies become too involved in the hurly-burly of routine politics, they will eventually appear to their own members and to the general public as special pleaders for ideological causes or even as appendages to transitory political factions.

# 4

# The Religious Right Has Too Much Political Influence

## Jim Wallis, interviewed by Michael Lumsden

*Jim Wallis is the editor of* Sojourners *magazine and the author of* God's Politics: Why the Right Gets It Wrong and the Left Doesn't Get It. *Michael Lumsden is an editorial fellow at* Mother Jones *magazine.*

The Republicans won the 2004 presidential election in large part because they understand how to talk about moral values and religious issues. However, religious fundamentalists on the Right have limited the national conversation about values to minor issues. They are neglecting to address more important issues, such as poverty. Liberals need to begin talking about these significant issues in moral and religious terms if they are to win an election and help address the concerns of most Americans.

To say, as some have, that the 2004 presidential election was won and lost on "moral values" is probably an overstatement. It's nevertheless true that among church-going, God-fearing types who think the country has lost its moral bearings, George W. Bush enjoyed vastly more support than did his rival, John Kerry. Is there a lesson here for the Democrats?

Yes, there is, according to Jim Wallis, editor of the leftish religious magazine *Sojourners*, whose new book, *God's Politics: Why the Right Gets It Wrong and the Left Doesn't Get It*, argues that

Democrats, if they ever want to win an election, must learn how to talk about moral values, indeed, to talk the *language* of moral values, in a way that remains true to the party's principles.

The American Right has been able to define "moral values" narrowly, almost exclusively in terms of wedge issues like abortion and gay marriage. It doesn't have to be this way, Wallis argues. Drawing on more than 30 years of work combating poverty, as well as an intimate knowledge of the Bible, Wallis, an evangelical Christian, argues that moral values encompass actions and attitudes toward a host of issues, including poverty, the environment, criminal justice and war.

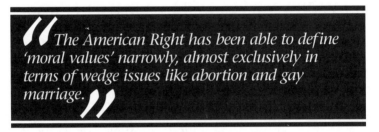

*The American Right has been able to define 'moral values' narrowly, almost exclusively in terms of wedge issues like abortion and gay marriage.*

Through a conversational combination of first-person stories, news analysis, statistics and old fashion preaching (on the written page), Wallis paints a very different picture of what religion means than the one President Bush and many of his supporters have in mind.

His message seems to be resonating with Americans from across the political spectrum. Published by HarperSanFrancisco late in January [2004], it is now fifth on the *New York Times* bestseller list. [In the spring of 2005], Wallis has been traveling the country to promote *God's Politics*. Speaking in churches, bookstores and on radio and television talk shows, Wallis says he is witnessing what could be the birth of a new movement that challenges the hold the Right has had on religion and morality for decades. In San Francisco recently, he dropped by to speak with MotherJones.com.

## The Right's Moral-Values Strategy

MotherJones.com: *The subtitle of your book is "Why the Right Gets It Wrong and the Left Doesn't Get It." What does the Right get wrong?*

Jim Wallis: The Right is comfortable with the language of religion, values, God talk. So much so that they sometimes claim to own that territory. Or own God. But then they narrow every-thing down to one or two issues: abortion and gay marriage.

I am an evangelical Christian, and I can't ignore thousands of verses in the Bible on [another] subject, which is poverty. I say at every stop, "Fighting poverty's a moral value, too." There's a whole generation of young Christians who care about the environment. That's their big issue. Protecting God's cre-ation, they would say, is a moral value, too. And, for a growing number of Christians, the ethics of war—how and when we go to war, whether we tell the truth about going to war—is a reli-gious and moral issue as well.

I think the Right has made a serious mistake in adopting a moral-values strategy, because they're winning in the short run. [But] in the long run, they're going to lose this debate be-cause they won't be able to restrict it to two issues. Once you open that door to a values conversation, it's going to undercut a right-wing economic agenda, which values wealth over work and favors the rich over the poor, or resorts to war as the first resort and not the last. To quote the White House, when it comes to moral values in this discussion, I say, "Bring it on!" Let's have the conversation, because the Right's going to lose this debate in the end. But not if the Left doesn't even get in the conversation.

*The Right has made a serious mistake in adopting a moral-values strategy, because they're winning in the short run. [But] in the long run, they're going to lose.*

*Is that what you mean when you say the Left doesn't get it?*
[Democrats] forget their own progressive history. Every ma-jor social movement in our history was fueled in large part by religion and faith. Abolitionism, women's suffrage, child labor law, and most famously, civil rights. Where would we be if the Reverend Dr. Martin Luther King Jr. had kept his faith to him-self? Here's a party that was vitally connected to the civil rights movement, led by black churches, now has driven so far [away], they're successfully portrayed by the Right as a secular party hostile to religion.

I think people who are religious or, say, even spiritual, have not felt like there's much of a home on the Left. That's at least a huge political concern. Even those who aren't religious need to respect people of faith. The connection the world's waiting for is to connect the hunger for spirituality with passion for social change. Because spirituality, when it isn't disciplined by social justice, in an affluent society, becomes narcissistic. We buy the books, we buy the tapes. We hear the guru speaker. Barnes & Noble has a whole wall of how to be spiritual, balanced, healed, whole. Spirituality becomes a commodity to be bought and sold. So spirituality has to be disciplined by social justice.

## The Left's Big Mistake

*And the Left's big mistake is that it has ignored that potential?*

Not just ignored; they've ceded the territory. They've ignored it at their peril and they've turned it over so that the Right gets to say, "Okay, we'll define it our way. Abortion, gay marriage. That's it. That's all. Nothing else."

*What would you say to what you call in the book "secular fundamentalists" who say, "I don't want anything to do with religion, and I don't want my politics or my party to have anything to do with religion either?"*

I don't call all secular people "secular fundamentalists." At every book stop, people say, "I'm secular; I'm an agnostic. Thank you for making me included tonight. I feel spiritually inspired, but I'm not religious. But I care about moral values." So, to those people I would say, "You know, you can be who you are, but just respect people who are people of faith and include [them] in the movement." To the secular fundamentalists who want to exclude any religion, I would say, "Do you want to lose every election for the rest of your life? Get smart. Remember progressive history." We all have an investment in our politics having a moral compass.

## How Religion Should Influence Politics

*In the book you say that it's not a matter of whether religion should influence politics, it's a matter of how.*

Yeah. This is America. This is the most religious nation on the face of the earth. Religion will be a factor in our public life. The founders wanted to separate church and state not to diminish the role of religion but to strengthen it. Europe has a state church framework and religion has almost no influence.

Here, where it's separated, it's more dependent and more vital, and stronger. The founders thought strong religion was a factor in the political health of the nation.

I say in the book how [Abraham] Lincoln gets this right, that you don't invoke God's blessing on the nation's policies. You don't say, "God is on our side." That leads to all the worst stuff in politics: triumphalism, hubris, bad foreign policy. If you worry that you are on God's side, that leads to humility and reflection, accountability, maybe even penitence—the missing values in politics.

King did it best: Bible in one hand, Constitution in the other. He never said, "I'm religious, so I get to win." He didn t say, "God spoke to me, and I have the fix for Social Security." He said, "I'm motivated by my faith, but I've got to persuade the public on the basis not of religion but of the common good."

*You don't say, 'God is on our side.' That leads to all the worst stuff in politics.*

*And nowhere in the book do you say that people need to get religion.*

In a funny way, I say both parties need to get religion on poverty. This is the big issue on God's heart, if we take the Bible seriously. Three million people living on less than $2 a day. Thirty thousand children dying every single day of what I call a silent tsunami—nobody pays attention to it.

The Right is attacking me for trying to help the Democrats get religious language so they can win an election. I say to Democrats when they call, "If you want Bible verses and cheap God-talk, I'm not really interested. This isn't going to be a sprint for you, but a marathon. Not a forum, but a long-term conversation." I'm interested in content more than language. What is the content of our politics? If getting religion means caring about poverty, then I want both parties to do that. [And for President Bush], I'd like to see some real serious commitment to poverty reduction both at home and around the world. I'd like to see him do the right thing. But so far, it's faith-based initiatives over here and a budget over here and there's no commitment to poverty whatsoever. . . .

*You mentioned in the book a poll that came out shortly after the election that said the majority of Americans wanted to hear about poverty.*

"What is the greatest moral crisis facing America?" is the poll. . . . Sixty-four percent said either greed and materialism or poverty and economic justice. And I think about 16 percent, abortion, and 11 percent or less, gay marriage. So when the question was asked straight up, moral values, that's what happened. . . .

What if we had a candidate who spoke to the issues of economic justice as a moral value? I think there'd be a deep resonance among American people. Democrats haven't made poverty a moral issue in years.

*So you think it was more the party not heeding the issue than the citizens?*

Absolutely. I'm out in the country all the time now; this is a big, big issue. This is a big issue for religious and non-religious people. Poverty could be the thing that calls us together across our political dividing lines. But you need political leaders who articulate that and say why this is connected to our faith, our humanity, and our security. . . .

I remember [journalist] Bill O'Reilly one night was yelling at me about [America's war with] Iraq. I said, "Bill, what would Jesus do? Can you imagine him climbing into the cockpit of a B-52 and dropping a load of bombs over Baghdad?" And Bill said, "Well Jesus would surely want to protect the American people." And I said, "Really? What about the Iraqis?" "Well, well, them, too." Once you start talking about this in a religious frame, it's troubling.

The Republicans will not hold [Bush] accountable to the biblical prophets when they think all the issues are about abortion, and the Democrats don't even know the language. He gets away with it. There's got to be a progressive religious response to Bush that says, "We don't quibble with your piety, but we challenge your theology." There is no American exceptionalism in the Bible. The Gospel is uneasy with empire—except American empire?

## A New Dialogue on Faith in Politics

*And in your travels you've seen that kind of response to Bush growing up from the grassroots?*

It's become a national town meeting. Folks who've been coming out feel that when faith is talked about in the media or the White House it's not their faith. It's always this narrow, either Religious Right or this White House religion, and I think people are finding their own voice and their own faith in the safe space of a discussion about a book. There are evangelicals, Catholics, mainline, black churches, Jews, Muslims, young people who say they're spiritual but not religious, agnostics who say they're secular but care about moral politics.

*Yet even if there is all that energy, unless it's organized and geared towards a goal . . .*

Well, the conversation back around my shop is, "What do we do with this?" This isn't just about selling books now. This is about how to build a movement on the back of a book tour. The story now is not the book, but the tour. Why are so many people at bookstores?

We're getting 400 in Dayton, Ohio, and Austin, Texas, and Wichita, Kan. Also in Philadelphia and Boston. They're sitting on the floor. In Los Angeles, it was pouring rain. A thousand people showed up. It's this buzzing thing, which means that something is needing to be expressed.

I'm getting 30 new speaking invitations every day. There are a lot of young, articulate spokespeople who ought to be out in the churches speaking, so we're going to create a speakers bureau and then move these invitations out to this new generation of young women, young men who have a lot to say.

I think it's less about my voice than [the people's]. They don't feel their voice has been represented in the conversation. And this is a chance to be heard. The good news is that the monologue of the Religious Right is now over and a new dialogue is finally beginning.

# 5

# The Religious Right Is Unfairly Criticized

## Paul Marshall

*Paul Marshall is a senior fellow at Freedom House's Center for Religious Freedom and the author of many books on religion and politics.*

After the 2004 presidential election, which George W. Bush won due in part to votes from religious conservatives, many political pundits went too far in their criticism of the Religious Right, some of them comparing Christian fundamentalists with Islamic terrorists. In doing so, these critics revealed their ignorance and religious intolerance. The world is full of religious extremists who harm no one and make a positive contribution to society, and secular pundits would benefit from learning about these groups.

The aftermath of the [2004 presidential] election brought a belated realization that President [George W.] Bush's victory was based in large part on increased evangelical turnout. Hence, predictably, committed religion is again an incendiary political topic, and again it is mindlessly stereotyped as "fundamentalism" and "religious extremism," characterized by closed-minded certitude—and, thus, the mirror image of Islamist extremism.

## Equating Fundamentalism with Terrorism

Three writers preached petulant sermons on the matter on the same *New York Times* op-ed page two days after the election.

Maureen Dowd called for George W. Bush's excommunication for promoting "a jihad in America so he can fight one in Iraq." Thomas Friedman condemned as apostates from America those "Christian fundamentalists" who "promote divisions and intolerance at home and abroad." Garry Wills, ever inquisitorial, demanded "where else" but in America "do we find fundamentalist zeal, a rage at secularity, religious intolerance, fear of and hatred for modernity?" Can't guess? "We find it in the Muslim world, in [terrorist group] al Qaeda, in [former Iraqi president] Saddam Hussein's Sunni loyalists"—and, writes Wills, Americans fear "jihad, no matter whose zeal is being expressed." Meanwhile, Ellen Goodman conjures up apocalyptic visions of a "country racked by the fundamentalist religious wars we see across the world," and Sean Wilentz anathematizes "the religious fanaticism that has seized control of the federal government."

> *A large slice of the punditocracy apparently believes with all its heart and mind and soul and strength that committed religion is akin to Islamist terrorism.*

Of course, people say silly things in a bleak post-election dawn. But similar litanies were recited during the campaign. [Former *New York Times* executive editor] Howell Raines portrayed "God's people" as seeking to enact "theologically based cultural norms." [Democratic Senator] Joe Biden pronounced a "death struggle between freedom and radical fundamentalism." [2000 Democratic presidential nominee] Al Gore pilloried Bush's faith as "the same fundamentalist impulse that we see in Saudi Arabia, in Kashmir, and in religions around the world." [*American Prospect* national editor] Robert Reich pontificated: "Terrorism itself is not the greatest danger we face," the "true battle" is with "those who believe that truth is revealed through Scripture and religious dogma." Bruce Bartlett, who served in the Reagan and Bush I administrations, reportedly averred that Bush II understands Islamic terrorists "because he's just like them," and has visions of a Manichean "battle . . . between modernists and fundamentalists, pragmatists and true believers, reason and religion."

Well, people say silly things in the frenzy of a campaign,

too. But these rants express something far deeper than political frustration: A large slice of the punditocracy apparently believes with all its heart and mind and soul and strength that committed religion is akin to Islamist terrorism.

After [terrorists attacked the United States on September 11, 2001], the noted [University of] Oxford scientist Richard Dawkins declaimed, "To fill a world with religion, or religions of the Abrahamic kind, is like littering the streets with loaded guns. Do not be surprised if they are used." Thomas Friedman preached, "World War III is a battle against . . . a view of the world . . . that my faith must remain supreme and can be affirmed and held passionately only if all others are negated. That's bin Ladenism [religious extremism]." [*New Republic* senior editor] Andrew Sullivan worried that "there is something inherent in religious monotheism that lends itself to this kind of terrorist temptation." [Political writer] Michael Lind announced that the Moral Majority and Christian Coalition have a "fundamentalist ideology . . . essentially identical to that of the Muslim extremists."

## Intolerance and Hypocrisy

What should be said about such dogmatic assertions, delivered with a finality that no pope or Baptist preacher would wish to match? Well, for starters, that they are intolerant, hypocritical, and wrong.

In claiming that monotheism and reliance on revelation are necessarily terroristic, these secular pundits condemn Christians, Jews, Jehovah's Witnesses, Unitarians, Sabeans, and Bahais, to name a few, along with George Washington, James Madison, and a host of other Founding Fathers, as inherently violent. Notice, however, that the condemnation extends also to the revealed monotheistic religion of Islam—and no one objects. Yet when [evangelical ministers] Jerry Falwell and Franklin Graham said that violence is inherent in Islam, they were pilloried by respectable opinion. These days, religious intolerance and theological illiteracy are far more conspicuous in the pages of the *New York Times* than among most southern fundamentalists.

There is also hypocrisy and self-contradiction. Friedman seems blissfully unaware that, even as he condemns others for holding out their particular faith as supreme, he is asserting the supremacy of his own passionately held view. His secularist critique attempts the miraculous combination of denouncing others' faith while attacking those who denounce others' faith. Do not try this trick at home. It should be attempted only by seasoned professionals who lack any capacity for self-criticism or even self-awareness.

> *Religious intolerance and theological illiteracy are far more conspicuous in the pages of the* New York Times *than among most southern fundamentalists.*

However, one can be intolerant and hypocritical—and also correct. The most important thing about these fulminations is that they are utterly, flat out, dead wrong.

## Defining "Fundamentalist"

Take the vacuous term "fundamentalist." Despite academic efforts to give it content, in practice the word signifies only "someone firmly committed to religious views I do not like." It's an epithet depicting people as abject objects to be labeled rather than listened to, dismissed rather than engaged in discussion.

It originated as a description of a series of Christian booklets called "The Fundamentals" published between 1910 and 1915 and focused on the nature of biblical criticism. They did not spring from the American South. Canadians, usually Episcopalians, wrote many of them, with additional contributors from Germany, Scotland, Ireland, and England. The first, on "The History of the Higher Criticism," was by Canon Dyson Hague, lecturer in liturgics and ecclesiology, Wycliffe College, Toronto, and examining chaplain to the (Anglican) bishop of Huron. It was followed by "The Bible and Modern Criticism" by F. Bettex, D.D., professor emeritus, Stuttgart, Germany.

The author of "Christ and Criticism" was Sir Robert Anderson, KCB, LLD. As a Knight Commander of the Bath (the third-highest British order of chivalry), he seems a far cry from the fundamentalists [that political commentator] H.L. Mencken vilified in the 1920s as "halfwits," "yokels," "rustic ignoramuses," "anthropoid rabble," and "gaping primates of the upland valleys," or even the people the *Washington Post* maligned 70 years

34

later as "largely poor, uneducated, and easy to command."

My work monitoring religious freedom and religious persecution around the world often brings me into contact with "fundamentalists" and "religious extremists." Some of them are indeed the monsters that secularists portray: I have seen enough prisons, killing fields, and bodies, lost enough friends, colleagues, and cases, and fallen asleep in tears on enough silent nights, to have few illusions about the terrors produced by perverted religion (or, for that matter, perverted secularism, which in the last century piled up vastly more corpses than did religious extremism).

## The Benefits of Religious Extremism

But there are also "religious extremists" I remember fondly. One I had the privilege of meeting believes he is the reincarnation of generations of religious leaders and was destined to lead his people. I don't share his views, but I find him wise, with a delightful sense of humor. He is the Dalai Lama.

Jehovah's Witnesses annoy many people by ringing our doorbells while we're having dinner. But the growth of religious freedom in almost every Western country owes much to the Witnesses' peaceful quest to be allowed to be conscientious objectors to military service.

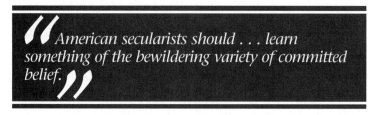

*American secularists should . . . learn something of the bewildering variety of committed belief.*

There were Trappist nuns in Java, committed to a life of silence on the slopes of a volcano. It surprised me that they were a major source of information about what really goes on in Indonesia, that land of shadows. But, as the mother superior, a New Yorker, explained, "We can't speak, but we can sure read, watch, and listen. If you don't speak, you'd be amazed how much you can learn." No wonder she left Manhattan.

The Dervishes in Turkey, Sufi Muslims, combine their strange, ecstatic, whirling dance with ecumenical spirituality and uncommon grace at being treated as a tourist attraction. Some of their neighbors, Turkish Christians, are reviving the ascetic practice of living, like Simon Stylites, on top of poles. Not my cup of tea, but they're not hurting anyone.

The Amish are as "fanatical" about their religion as Americans get. They use no electricity, no cars, no colorful clothing, and are fierce pacifists, as are many other "fundamentalists." I'm still tempted to go back with them.

Then there are the practitioners of Falun Gong, the Hindu Shankaracharya of Puri, the Hasidim, and so many others with views that would drive American secularists up the wall. All are resolutely peaceful. I disagree with most, and have spent many happy, and frequently frustrating, hours with them discussing life, the universe, and everything. But I have never felt the slightest need to attack them, nor they me.

In the face of this range of beliefs, it is well nigh meaningless to define [al Qaeda leader Osama] bin Laden and his ilk as "fundamentalists" or "religious extremists." He may be both, but so are billions of peaceful and gentle people.

The difference is obvious: The key is not bin Laden's conviction or certitude, but the content of his creed. We are opposed not to "religious extremists" per se, but only to the type of religious extremists who believe in flying planes into buildings and beheading "infidels."

In doing so we are allied with, and in large part defended by, people secularists label "religious extremists." This includes a significant proportion of the American military, especially the Marine Corps, who are, by most accounts, more evangelical than the population at large. Are the *New York Times* et al. seriously suggesting that the war on Islamofascism is at root a war on people like those in the U.S. armed forces?

In place of such fatuities, American secularists should stop trying to hitch their postmodern prejudices to the war on Islamist terrorism and instead stoop to learn something of the bewildering variety of committed belief. Their insistence on lumping together all religious convictions is bigotry, and error, fundamentally so.

# 6

# The United States Should Maintain Strict Separation Between Church and State

## Ron Flowers

*Ron Flowers is a professor at Texas Christian University and the author of* History of Religion in America.

Separation of church and state means that the government may not impose religion on the public, but also that individuals may not use the state as an instrument to practice religion. This system is different from that of many other countries, where multiple religions flourish but one or more receive support from the government. Many religious Americans feel that strict enforcement of separation between church and state is hostile to religion, but actually strict separation has allowed religions to flourish without interference from the government. People who oppose separation of church and state usually want the government to promote religion, which would be unconstitutional.

R ecently I received this story by e-mail:

They walked in tandem, each of the 93 students filing into the already crowded auditorium. With rich maroon gowns flowing and the traditional caps, they looked almost as grown up as they felt.

Ron Flowers, "Separation of Church and State—It's Nothing to Sneeze At," *Church and State,* vol. 57, May 2004. Copyright © 2004 by the Americans United for Separation of Church and State. Reproduced by permission.

Dads swallowed hard behind broad smiles, and moms freely brushed away tears.

This class would not pray during the commencement—not by choice but because of a recent court ruling prohibiting it. The principal and several students were careful to stay within the guidelines allowed by the ruling.

They gave inspirational and challenging speeches, but no one mentioned divine guidance and no one asked for blessings on the graduates or their families.

The speeches were nice, but they were routine—until the final speech received a standing ovation.

A solitary student walked proudly to the microphone. He stood still and silent for just a moment, and then, it happened. The other 92 students, every single one of them, suddenly Sneezed!!!!

The student on stage simply looked at the audience and said, "God bless you, each and every one of you!" And he walked off-stage.

The audience exploded into applause. The graduating class had found a unique way to invoke God's blessing on their future with or without the court's approval!

Isn't this a wonderful story?

Pass it on to all your friends.

No, it is not a wonderful story. . . .

The story is correct that the prohibition on commencement prayers in public schools is based on a 1992 Supreme Court decision, *Lee v. Weisman.*

The opinion was written by Anthony Kennedy, who was appointed by President Ronald Reagan and is one of the more conservative justices on the Supreme Court. But the decision was not designed to be hostile to religion.

## Religious Freedom vs. Religious Toleration

The decision recognized that our society is religiously pluralistic. Not everyone believes in God the same way; some do not believe at all. But they are all Americans. They are all entitled to religious freedom. They are all entitled to not have the government or any instrument of government impose religion upon them.

The sneeze story implies that all the members of the graduating class participated in eliciting the blessing of God. Perhaps so. But that would not always be the case.

Remember that peer pressure in junior high and high school is enormous. Students who may have objections—religiously based objections—to prayer in classrooms or commencements may find it very difficult to express those against the majority.

But, you may say, in this country the majority rules.

Not in constitutional matters.

As Justice Robert Jackson eloquently said in 1943 in *West Virginia Board of Education v. Barnette:* "One's right to life, liberty, and property, to free speech, a free press, freedom of worship and assembly, and other fundamental rights may not be submitted to vote; they depend on the outcome of no elections."

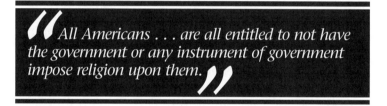

*All Americans . . . are all entitled to not have the government or any instrument of government impose religion upon them.*

The precious concept of religious freedom means that every person in this country is free to practice his or her religion. But the idea of separation of church and state means that one may not use the state as an instrument to practice that religion. And that means that all Americans, including students in public schools, are entitled to not have the government or any agent of government impose religion upon them.

Let us step back from this specific issue to look at a larger principle: the difference between toleration and freedom—toleration of religion and freedom of religion.

We frequently say that the Founders of our nation created a system of toleration of religion. But they did not. They created a system of religious freedom.

What is the difference?

Toleration means that the government regulates the religious situation. It usually means that a particular religion or religious tradition is favored, but others are allowed to exist. The others may even be allowed wide latitude for religious belief and practice. But the concept of toleration still holds the power in the government to determine the religious situation.

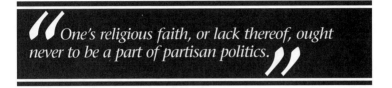

*One's religious faith, or lack thereof, ought never to be a part of partisan politics.*

Many countries have this system. In England, the Church of England is the established church. It receives financial and political favors from the government that other religious groups do not receive. Although other religious groups may have wide leeway to practice their faiths, the government still has the power to limit their religious freedom—or, indeed, to take away their permission to exist.

Religious freedom is different from toleration. Religious freedom means that the government has no say in whether a religion may exist in the country. It means that the government has no say in what a religion teaches or how it is practiced, with the proviso that religious practice may not harm the public welfare.

The Founders of America created a Constitution of limited government. In doing so, they gave us religious freedom. When they wrote in the First Amendment that "Congress shall make no law respecting an establishment of religion, or prohibiting the free exercise thereof," they meant that religion should be free from government support or control.

That is, they also meant that government should step back so religious people and groups could be free to practice their faiths as they choose. That means that groups or individuals may not use the machinery of the government to practice their religion. There cannot be any governmentally enforced expression of religion, such as prayer in public school commencements.

## No Religious Test for Public Office

America's Founders also wrote in Article VI of the Constitution that "no religious Test shall ever be required as a Qualification to any Office or public Trust under the United States."

In this [2004] election season, considerable notice has been made of the role of religion in the campaign. But the Founders' cautionary note in the Constitution is a reminder that one's religious faith, or lack thereof, ought never to be a part of partisan politics. God does not favor one party over another.

Many argue that they want their leaders to be people of principle and morality. That is certainly a fair-enough expectation. The presumption is that those principles and morality will be derived from religion. That is a logical assumption also. We consequently want our leaders and candidates for leadership to be religious.

But the Founders remembered that in colonial America one could not hold public office if he were not a member of the established church. That certainly limited the possibility for a wide range of qualified candidates.

So the Founders eliminated the possibility of a national established religion in the First Amendment and forbade religious tests of qualification for public office in Article VI.

Both candidates and office holders have the right to be religious and to express their religiosity. But the prohibition against religious tests for public office is a reminder that God does not play partisan politics.

And it is a cautionary note that politicians should not use religion against their opponents. Religiosity as a political tool can so easily lead to self-righteousness.

But you may respond to all this by concluding that separation of church and state is hostile to religion. For the Constitution to forbid religious tests for public office and to not allow government sponsorship of or mandate for religious ceremonies in government institutions such as public schools must mean that separation of church and state is hostile to religion.

## Separation Benefits Religion

People often ask me why, given that I am a Christian and an ordained minister, I am such an advocate for separation of church and state.

The answer, of course, is: because I am a Christian and an ordained minister.

I take my faith very seriously. For faith to be insulated from the corroding influences of government and politics is a good thing. Remember that part of the concept of the separation of church and state is the Founders' explicit command that government should not prohibit the free exercise of religion.

Separation of church and state enables faith to flourish without interference from government power. Separation of church and state has allowed religion to be as vibrant, dynamic and lively as it is in American society.

To be sure, government may not use religion as a tool to get its way with the people. It is illegitimate for government to advance or inhibit religion.

Separation demands that government get out of the way and let people respond to the divine as they will. The people do that, and in America religion is a major part of the culture. Separation of church and state is not hostile to religion but rather is the enabler for religions to grow and prosper in America.

But many in our time are fearful of true freedom. They are not willing to trust the people to practice their religion as they choose. Rather, they want the government to somehow promote religion.

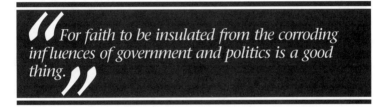

*For faith to be insulated from the corroding influences of government and politics is a good thing.*

So we have presidential executive orders to provide government money to charitable programs operated by religious institutions. We have legislatures across the country passing laws and resolutions to post the Ten Commandments in public buildings. We have continual efforts, including bills in Congress to amend the Constitution, to promote prayer and devotionals in public schools. On and on.

## Trivializing Religion

But there are at least two problems with this trend. One is that in the effort to have government-promoted religion, religion is often trivialized. For example, in many of the Ten Commandments displays, in the effort to avoid being an obvious Establishment Clause violation, other famous sayings are often added. These are bits from the Declaration of Independence, the Code of Hammurabi or Abraham Lincoln's second inaugural address. They are all fine sayings in and of themselves. But it is clear that they are providing cover for the Ten Commandments. There is a bit of intellectual dishonesty going on there.

What we really have is a kind of theological bait-and-switch operation. Rather than be content with aggressively teaching the Ten Commandments in their churches, synagogues and homes, many are more interested in playing theological hide-and-seek to sneak the Commandments onto public buildings and monuments.

Another example of the trivialization of religion is the story with which I began. In the attempt to be able to get a prayer into the commencement, albeit ever so brief a prayer, someone went to great lengths to organize all 93 seniors and coordinate the great sneeze. Then, responding to this stimulus like Pavlov's dog, a person was able to say: "God bless you, each and every one of you!"

It reminds me of what we used to sing as junior high kids at church camp: "Hooray for Jesus. Hooray for Jesus. Someone in the crowd's shouting, 'Hooray for Jesus.'" A statement of belief, but bordering on the trite. Hardly profound theology.

Finally, the attempt to get the state to promote religion has great potential to harm the church. I am amazed that some ministers, TV religious personalities and even denominational leaders are so eager to get the government to do the work of the church. In the interest in getting religion more into the public life of the country, they run the risk of marginalizing the church. The more the state does the work of the church, the less relevant the church will become.

Although it probably was unwitting on their part, the Founders of this country gave religious people the ideal methodology for vital, energetic, robust, vigorous religious institutions. They gave us the separation of church and state with its corollary: religious freedom. Free from government dominance or interference, churches could flourish in this country, and they have.

But now, in these latter days, in the interest of trying to improve public morality, many believe that the church must utilize the state to get its way with the people. That is a prescription to make the church subservient to the state, to marginalize it and make it less dynamic.

Supreme Court Justice Hugo Black once wrote that separation of church and state "stands as an expression of principle on the part of the Founders of our Constitution that religion is too personal, too sacred, too holy to permit its 'unhallowed perversion' by a civil magistrate."

Isn't that a wonderful concept?

Pass it on to all your friends.

# 7

# Separation Between Church and State Does Not Mean That Religious Views Should Be Excluded from Politics

Edward F. Harrington

*Edward F. Harrington is United States Senior District Judge for the District of Massachusetts.*

The idea that political figures should not be influenced by their religious beliefs, or that religious views should not inform public policy debates, is misguided. People who hold this view often invoke the metaphor of a wall between church and state. However, that metaphor was originally coined to convey the idea that religion should be protected from government control—not that government should be protected from citizens with religious beliefs. Rather than calling for the regulation or curtailment of religious speech, the First Amendment encourages religious expression and protects it from government control.

The metaphor "wall of separation" has long been used by some political figures and commentators as a call to exclude the teachings of religion and religiously rooted morality from participation in political debate concerning public policy.

Edward F. Harrington, "The Metaphorical Wall," *America,* vol. 192, January 17, 2005, p. 10. Copyright © 2005 by America Press, www.americamagazine.org. All rights reserved. Reproduced by permission.

44

Those who espouse such moral teachings in an attempt to shape the public agenda are scorned and ridiculed for infecting the public forum with their sectarian and, by implication, un-American discourse.

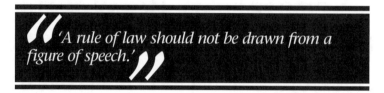

*'A rule of law should not be drawn from a figure of speech.'*

But as Justice [Stanley] Reed of the U.S. Supreme Court stated in *McCollum v. Board of Education* (1948), "a rule of law should not be drawn from a figure of speech." The idea of "separation of church and state" was never meant to protect the state. Rather, it was designed to protect the religious rights of the people from the incursion of the government.

## Origins of the Term

The metaphor "wall of separation" was coined by Roger Williams in the 17th century, before the colonies became independent and before the ratification of the United States Constitution. Williams was the pioneer of religious freedom and defender of the liberty of conscience. He believed no civil government could compel adherence to a religious doctrine without endangering free will. He imagined a "wall of separation between the garden of the church and the wilderness of the world."

Thomas Jefferson returned to this imagery as president. In 1802, in a private letter to the Danbury (Conn.) Baptist Association, he wrote, "Believing with you that religion is a matter which lies solely between man and his God, that he owes account to none other for his faith or worship, that the legislative powers of government reach actions only, and not opinions, I contemplate with sovereign reverence that act of the whole American people which declared that their legislature should 'make no law respecting an establishment of religion, or prohibiting the free exercise thereof,' thus building a wall of separation between church and state." As with Williams, the metaphor "wall of separation" was used by Jefferson as a shorthand formula to endorse religious liberty against the power and control of the state. The term served solely as an aid to religious belief.

# The Bill of Rights and the First Amendment

The principles of religious liberty that Jefferson extols as "the most inalienable and sacred of all human rights" find their ultimate source in the Bill of Rights of the U.S. Constitution. These first 10 amendments were enacted to secure certain fundamental individual rights, including the rights to religion. Jefferson writes to James Madison, "A bill of rights is what the people are entitled to against every government on earth." So, too, in the *West Virginia State Board of Education v. Barnette* (1945), Justice [Robert] Jackson states that "The very purpose of a Bill of Rights was . . . to place [certain subjects] beyond the reach of majorities and officials and to establish them as legal principles. . . ." The Bill of Rights thus was designed not to shield the state and its policies and practices from the exercise of those individual rights by its citizens, but rather to protect the exercise of those individual rights from infringement by the state. The Bill of Rights was erected as a bulwark, a "wall," as it were, against the state.

The individual's rights to religion are the very first rights defined and secured by the First Amendment. The amendment begins, "Congress shall make no law respecting an establishment of religion, or prohibiting the free exercise thereof." The free speech and free press clauses come only after this.

*A citizen's advocacy of a political view infused by his faith is protected and encouraged by both the free exercise and free speech clauses of the First Amendment.*

The no-establishment clause says that government shall not establish a religion, nor enforce its observance by law, nor compel any citizen to worship in a manner contrary to his conscience. This clause was designed to prohibit the establishment of a state-sponsored church or a national religion and prevents the state from giving any religious denomination a preferred legal status. The free exercise of religion clause that follows bans the state from restraining a citizen's unfettered choice to believe the tenets of his faith and to worship in accordance with his conscience. Each of these clauses reinforces the other; the freedom of religious expression finds its logical corollary in the prohibition of a state-sponsored religion.

The New York Constitutional Ratifying Convention set forth this doctrine of individual religious liberty in succinct and lucid language: "That the people have an equal, natural, and unalienable right freely and peacefully to exercise their religion according to the dictates of conscience; and no religious sect or society ought to be favored or established, by law, in preference to others." The First Amendment, then, is a barrier against the state, not against the people; it sets limits on governmental power and guarantees individual liberties, including religious liberty. It requires the state to be neutral in religious matters, to "keep its hands off" religious choices and leave decisions of conscience to the people.

## Religion and Public Policy Debate

Since the government is barred from curbing a citizen's exercise of his religious beliefs, ministers of religion of every creed and sect can freely engage in public debate in an endeavor to influence governmental policy in accordance with their religious-based moral values. The "wall of separation" permits maximum freedom to religious ideas and expression and deprives the state of any power to curtail that freedom. What is more, a citizen's advocacy of a political view infused by his faith is protected and encouraged by both the free exercise and free speech clauses of the First Amendment. The religious clauses of the First Amendment dictate a simple but profound injunction: Religion shall have the power to persuade; government shall lack the power to compel.

It is most crucial for the lasting vitality of individual liberties that the metaphorical "wall of separation" be understood in accordance with its historical and true meaning, and that religion be properly regarded as possessing rights with the same scope as the rights to speech and the rights of the press. No one has ever advanced the argument that the state and its policies and practices should be immune from the criticism and censure of free speech and free press, even when the exercise of such rights conveys mistakes of fact or errors in judgment or is actuated by bias or personal animosity. Neither should a figure of speech whose root meaning has become obscured over time be used to curtail religion, the first and most precious right of a free people. The very same "wall" that secures free speech and free press also defends the free exercise of religion against the state. It is the sole and organic source of each of these sacred individual liberties. The rostrum in the forum is open to all three.

A vibrant public policy can long endure only if grounded on such fundamental moral values as equality, fairness, freedom, love of neighbor and compassion for the poor, the sick and the aged. And morality is inseparable from the teachings of religion on the nature and condition of the human person and people's relationship to their Creator. The moral values of the great religious traditions, which have sustained and enriched world cultures through the ages, should not be exiled from the public square because of a metaphor whose true meaning has been distorted by some who possess an abiding hostility to religion's influence on the public agenda. The public square needs to hear the voices of a religiously based morality, so that public affairs may be nourished by their ideals of justice and equity. These ideals have inspired the struggle for emancipation of the slave, integration of the races and equality of the sexes.

# 8

# American Politics Is Dominated by Battles Between Religious and Secular Voters

## Louis Bolce and Gerald De Maio

*Louis Bolce and Gerald De Maio are professors of political science at the City University of New York.*

American politics is dominated by a war over religion. The mainstream media tend to emphasize one aspect of this division: that religious conservatives and fundamentalists vote Republican. An overlooked, relatively new force in U.S. politics is that of secularist voters, who have become an influential group within the Democratic Party. Secularists reject traditional religious values and are usually liberal voters who oppose conservatives on issues such as abortion and gay rights. However, secularists are also distinguished by their antipathy toward Christian fundamentalists and their belief that religious groups should not be involved in politics. Secularist voters are essentially anti-fundamentalist voters, and they threaten to make the Democratic Party be seen as hostile to religion.

Anyone who has followed American politics [since 1992] cannot help but feel some concern about the supposed fundamentalist Christian threat to democratic civility, pluralism, and tolerance. At the very least, the attentive citizen would find

Louis Bolce and Gerald De Maio, "Our Secularist Democratic Party," *Public Interest,* Fall 2002. Copyright © 2002 by National Affairs, Inc. Reproduced by permission of the authors.

it hard not to regard the cultural and political positions of fundamentalists as outside the mainstream, given the volume of media stories that have conveyed this point. At the same time, the media's obsession with politicized fundamentalism distracts public attention from the changing role of religion in political life today. In particular, the media overlooks the remarkable erosion of denominational boundaries that until a quarter century ago defined the religious dimension of partisan conflict, with Catholics, Jews, and southern evangelicals aligned with the Democratic party and nonsouthern white, mostly mainline Protestants forming the religious base of the Republicans. Also, the media mistakenly frames cultural conflict since the 1970s as entirely the result of fundamentalist revanchism. In so doing, the media ignores the growing influence of secularists in the Democratic party and obfuscates how their worldview is just as powerful a determinant of social attitudes and voting behavior as is a religiously traditionalist outlook. . . .

## The Origins of the Culture Wars

The "culture wars" is the controversial metaphor used to describe the restructuring of religious and cultural conflict in the United States since the 1960s. The thesis is most closely associated with sociologist James Davison Hunter, whose 1991 book *The Culture Wars* posited that "the dominant impulse at the present time is toward the polarization of a religiously informed public culture into distinct moral and religious camps." Hunter called these camps "orthodox" and "progressivist." On the orthodox side are persons who locate moral authority in a transcendent source, such as God or the Bible. Orthodox morality, according to Hunter, adheres to an absolute standard of right and wrong and is based on universalistic principles. Progressivists, in contrast, embrace a humanistic ethic drawn from reason, science, and personal experience. Progressivist moral rules are "loose-bounded," pluralistic, and relative to circumstance. This new cleavage cuts across the major American faith traditions and most denominations.

The two groups in the front lines of the culture wars are evangelical Christians, including fundamentalists, characterized by their high levels of religiosity and conservative attitudes on cultural issues, and secularists, who reject traditional religious values and tend to espouse liberal views on cultural and church-state issues. Much has been written in the popular

50

media about the traditionalist side and its alignment with the Republican party since the 1980s. Although considerable attention has been devoted to religious and cultural conflict in American political life, few in the mainstream media have acknowledged the true origins of this conflict—namely, the increased prominence of secularists within the Democratic party, and the party's resulting antagonism toward traditional values.

Secularists first appeared as a political force within a major party at the 1972 Democratic National Convention. Prior to then, neither party contained many secularists nor showed many signs of moral or cultural progressivism. Moreover, prior to the late 1960s, there was something of a tacit commitment among elites in both parties to the traditional Judeo-Christian teachings regarding authority, sexual mores, and the family. This consensus was shattered in 1972 when the Democratic party was captured by a faction whose cultural reform agenda was perceived by many (both inside and outside the convention) as antagonistic to traditional religious values. The political scientist Geoffrey Layman has defined this bloc, the largest in the party, as "secularists,"—that is, self-identified agnostics, atheists, and persons who never or seldom attend religious services. Over a third of white delegates fit this description, a remarkable figure considering that, according to James Davison Hunter, only about 5 percent of the population in 1972 could be described as secularists.

> *[Secularists'] worldview is just as powerful a determinant of social attitudes and behavior as is a religiously traditionalist outlook.*

Layman's research was based on the 1972–92 Convention Delegate Survey (CDS), the most comprehensive study to date of the political attitudes and religious orientations of national party convention delegates. Analyses of the 1972 CDS dataset by Jeane Kirkpatrick, and more recently by Layman, show that degree of religious commitment was among the most important characteristics distinguishing supporters from opponents of the progressivist planks in the platform relating to women's rights, abortion, alternative life styles, and the traditional family. Secularists strongly favored the progressivist positions; religiously traditional Democratic delegates opposed them. The differences over policies and candidates between traditionalist and secularist Democrats had less to do with disagreement over the future course of New Deal liberalism than with the divergent moral outlooks animating their competing worldviews.

> *" Few in the mainstream media have acknowledged the . . . increased prominence of secularists within the Democratic party. "*

The religious and cultural cleavages that roiled the Democrats in 1972 were nonexistent at the Republican convention, where mainline Protestants still dominated. The GOP [Republican] platform that year merely reiterated cultural positions the party had endorsed in past platforms, for example, support for school prayer and the Equal Rights Amendment. The Republicans, by default more than by overt action, became the traditionalist party. "The partisan differences that emerged in 1972," writes Layman in his book *The Great Divide*, "were not caused by any sudden increase in the religious and cultural traditionalism of the Republican activists but instead by the pervasive secularism and cultural liberalism of the Democratic supporters of [1972 presidential nominee] George McGovern."

## Secularists vs. the Faithful

The 1972 Democratic convention set in motion a political dynamic that continues to the present. The ascendancy of secularists in the Democratic party had long-term consequences for the relative attractiveness of each party for members of different religious groups. The Democratic party became more appealing to secularists and religious modernists and less attractive to traditionalists. The secularist putsch in the Democratic party had the opposite effect on its rival, which over time came to be seen as more hospitable to religious traditionalists and less appealing to more secular Republicans. What was at first an intraparty culture war among Democratic elites became by the 1980s an interparty culture war.

Interparty religious polarization was very apparent in the composition and attitudes of the delegates attending the 1992

Democratic and Republican conventions, events that launched what is now recognized as the first electoral culture war. According to CDS, 60 percent of first-time white delegates at the Democratic convention in New York City either claimed no attachment to religion or displayed the minimal attachment by attending worship services "a few times a year" or less. About 5 percent of first-time delegates at the Republican convention in Houston [Texas] identified themselves as secularists, a figure that had not budged for 20 years. Between 1972 and 1992, the percentage of nominal mainline Protestants among first-time Republican delegates declined from over one-third to one-fifth, while the proportion of religiously committed evangelical and fundamentalist delegates in this group tripled to 18 percent. Two-thirds of white Republican delegates attended religious services at least once a month, while only two of five white Democratic delegates demonstrated that level of commitment to their faiths.

> *Secularists . . . distinguished themselves from moderates and traditionalists by the antipathy they expressed toward Christian fundamentalists.*

Increased religious polarization can also be seen in the way Democratic and Republican delegates view various core constituent groups of the opposing party. Democratic and Republican activists in the CDS surveys were significantly more negative toward groups associated with the newer religious and cultural divisions in the electorate than toward groups associated with older political cleavages based on class, race, ethnicity, party, or ideology. In 1992, the average thermometer score of Republican delegates toward union leaders, liberals, blacks, Hispanics, and Democrats, for example, was 17 degrees warmer than their mean score toward feminists, environmentalists, and prochoice groups (44 degrees versus 27 degrees, respectively). Similarly, the mean thermometer score of Democratic delegates that year was 21 degrees warmer toward conservatives, the rich, big business, and Republicans than their average score toward prolife groups and Christian fundamentalists (34 degrees versus 13 degrees, respectively). Of the 18 groups tested by CDS, the most negatively rated group was Christian fundamentalists. Over half of Democratic delegates gave Christian fundamentalists the absolute minimum score they could, 0 degrees, and the average Democratic thermometer score toward this religious group was a very cold 11 degrees.

## A House Divided

To discover the extent to which the new, religious cleavage has expanded beyond party activists into the electorate, we classified ANES[1] respondents according to their attitudes toward scriptural authority and their levels of religiosity. Persons who did not exhibit the minimum of religiosity (i.e., those who rejected scriptural authority, had no religious affiliation, never attended religious services or prayed, and indicated that religion provided no guidance in their day-to-day lives) were coded as secularists. Respondents who exhibited the highest levels of faith and commitment (i.e., those who prayed and attended religious services regularly, accepted the Bible as divinely inspired, and said that religion was important to their daily lives) were coded as traditionalists. Persons who fell between these poles were classified as religious moderates. In 2000, about two-thirds of respondents fell into this last category, with the remaining respondents divided about evenly between secularists and traditionalists. (Since the culture wars are largely a clash in values among whites, we confined our analysis to white respondents in the ANES surveys.)

Answers to ANES surveys covering the past three presidential elections highlight two important aspects about the secularist worldview. First, it is associated with a relativistic outlook. Two-thirds of secularists in each of the surveys agreed with the statement that "we should adjust our views of right and wrong to changing moral standards," a perspective on morality with which traditionalists overwhelmingly disagreed. And second, secularism is no less powerful a determinant of attitudes on the contentious cultural issues than is religious traditionalism. In most instances, secularists consistently and lopsidedly embraced culturally progressivist positions. Traditionalists generally lined up on the opposite side, and religious moderates fell in between. Secularists were most distinct with respect to the coolness they displayed toward the traditional two-parent fam-

1. American National Election Study, a 2000 survey conducted by the Center for Political Studies at the University of Michigan

ily, their greater tolerance of marital infidelity, and their intense support for the prochoice position on abortion. Seven of ten secularists opposed any law restricting a woman's right to abortion, while majorities of moderates and traditionalists favored some restrictions on abortion. For example, over three-quarters of moderates and traditionalists approved of parental-consent laws and the banning of partial-birth abortion.

Secularists also distinguished themselves from moderates and traditionalists by the antipathy they expressed toward Christian fundamentalists (38 degrees on the thermometer scale) and their belief that the involvement of religious groups in politics is divisive and harmful for society. Traditionalists, on the other hand, were out of sync with the rest of the public with regard to their restrictive attitudes toward legalized abortion—most either wanted to ban the procedure altogether or favored limiting it to narrow circumstances such as rape, incest, or when the woman's life is in danger. Moreover, while most traditionalists favored allowing gays to serve in the military, they were distinct from the rest in their strong opposition to gay adoption.

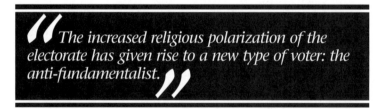

*The increased religious polarization of the electorate has given rise to a new type of voter: the anti-fundamentalist.*

Studies based on ANES survey data also show that the cultural attitudes of the electorate have become more polarized since the 1980s. But contrary to conventional wisdom, this increased cleavage had less to do with traditionalists becoming more conservative than with secularists (and to a lesser extent, religious moderates) embracing the progressivist positions held by liberal elites.

These sharp differences in moral and religious perspectives help to explain why religiously polarized party evaluations and voting behavior shot up during this period. In its election surveys, ANES includes an open-ended question: "Is there anything in particular that you like or (dislike) about the Republican or Democratic party?" Answers to these questions, which permit respondents to volunteer their own reasons for making judgments about a political party and its presidential candidates, show that cultural and religion-based evaluations have increased since the first Clinton election [in 1992]. Moreover during this time span secularists and traditionalists have voiced mirror-opposite "likes" and "dislikes" about the parties' stances toward "religious people," the "Christian Right," "abortion," "gay rights," "school prayer," and other cultural concerns. In the 2000 ANES survey, for example, secularists were nearly four times more likely to volunteer religion-based dislikes about groups and positions associated with the Republican party than were traditionalists, who in turn were four times more likely to voice cultural or religious reasons for disliking the Democratic party.

Secularists and traditionalists not only view the parties differently, but have increasingly become important voting blocs in the Democratic and Republican parties, respectively. One team of political scientists characterized the 1992 election alternatively as "the Year of the Evangelical" and the "Year of the Secular." The vote distribution of ANES respondents who indicated that they backed a major-party presidential candidate in the 1992 election supports this assertion. Secularists gave Clinton over three-quarters of their vote, while traditionalists favored President [George H.W.] Bush over Clinton by a margin of two to one. This polarized voting pattern continued through the 2000 presidential election.

In terms of their size and party loyalty, secularists today are as important to the Democratic party as another key Democratic constituency, organized labor. In the 2000 election, for example, both secularists and union members comprised about 16 percent of the white electorate, and both backed [Democratic nominee Al] Gore with two-thirds of their votes. The religious gap among white voters in the 1992, 1996, and 2000 presidential elections was more important than other demographic and social cleavages in the electorate; it was much larger than the gender gap and more significant than any combination of differences in education, income, occupation, age, marital status, and regional groupings. The importance of evangelicals to the ascendancy of the Republican party since the 1980s has been pointed out ad nauseam by media elites. But if the GOP can be labeled the party of religious conservatives, the Democrats, with equal validity, can be called the secularist party.

## The Anti-Fundamentalist Voter

The increased religious polarization of the electorate has given rise to a new type of voter: the anti-fundamentalist. We discovered this when we examined one group of ANES respondents: those who rated Christian fundamentalists 35 degrees or below on ANES's scale. We wanted to find out whether elite hostility to Christian fundamentalists, clearly apparent in the convention delegate surveys, had filtered into broader segments of the public. In ANES's 2000 survey, about a quarter of white respondents met the anti-fundamentalist criterion, rating fundamentalists 35 degrees or below. For comparison purposes, only 1 percent felt this antagonistic toward Jews and about 2.5 percent expressed this degree of hostility toward blacks and Catholics. ANES results indicate that antifundamentalism appears disproportionately among secularists, the highly educated, particularly those living in big cities, and persons who strongly favor legalized abortion and gay rights, oppose prayer in schools, and who, ironically, "strongly agree" that one should be tolerant of persons whose moral standards are different from one's own.

The results indicate that [since 1992] persons who intensely dislike fundamentalist Christians have found a partisan home in the Democratic party. Clinton captured 80 percent of these voters in his victories over President Bush in 1992 and over Senator Robert Dole four years later; Gore picked up 70 percent of the anti-fundamentalist vote in the 2000 election. One has to reach back to pre–New Deal America, when political divisions between Catholics and Protestants encapsulated local ethno-cultural cleavages over prohibition, immigration, public education, and blue laws [which prohibit certain activities on Sundays], to find a period when voting behavior was influenced by this degree of antipathy toward a religious group.

Yet it is not just their loyalty that makes anti-fundamentalists important to the Democratic coalition, but also the contribution they make to the total Democratic vote. According to ANES survey results, over a quarter of Clinton's white supporters in 1992 said that they intensely disliked Christian fundamentalists; in both 1996 and 2000, about a third of the total white Democratic presidential vote came from persons with these sentiments. During this era of religious polarization, Democratic presidential candidates have never captured a majority of the three-quarters of the white electorate who do not feel antipathy toward Christian fundamentalists. As a result, gaining solid support from anti-fundamentalist voters has become crucial to achieving victories at the national level. The upshot of these voting trends is that the Democrats today face electoral liabilities analogous but opposite to those of the Republicans. Just as Republicans need to win the evangelical-fundamentalist vote without scaring off religious moderates, so too must Democrats mobilize secularists and anti-fundamentalists without becoming too identified in public discourse as the party hostile to religion.

# 9

# American Politics Is Dominated by Battles Between Different Kinds of Religious Voters

## Hanna Rosin

*Hanna Rosin is a journalist who has written for the* New Republic, *the* Washington Post, *and the* Atlantic Monthly.

Despite claims by conservative public figures, the concept of a political split between religious and secularist voters is wrong. There are simply too few secular voters to constitute a bloc—only 5 percent of Americans say they do not believe in God or a higher power. Rather, America's political divide is between different types of religious voters: traditionalists, centrists, and modernists. Traditionalists are the most conservative and are often referred to as fundamentalists. Centrists wish to adapt religious beliefs to new times, and modernists want to abandon traditional doctrine. On political issues, traditionalists from different religions are more likely to agree with one another than with centrists or modernists from their own faith. The Republican Party has recognized this and has begun courting different kinds of traditionalists, who are now a strong force in American politics. Centrists and modernists, on the other hand, are less organized and are currently losing power within religious America.

Richard Land is gloating, and who can blame him? When I called him a few weeks after the 2004 election, he said he'd been driving around his home town of Nashville [Tennessee] with his cell phone ringing constantly, CNN on one line, *Time* magazine on the other—everyone wanting to ask the prominent Southern Baptist how his people had managed to win the election for George W. Bush. Yes, he told me, "we white evangelicals were the driving engine" of the president's victory. But then he veered into the kind of interview a quarterback gives in the locker room, in which he thanks the offensive line and the tight end and the coach and, well, really the whole team for bringing it home. "You'd be shocked," Land said, "at the number of Catholics who voted for this president. You'd be shocked at the number of Orthodox Jews, even observant Jews. This was a victory for all people of traditional moral values."

"Moral values." The phrase has turned into the hanging chad of the 2004 election, the cliché no one takes seriously. Do the debates over Iraq and the economy not involve moral values? Is everyone in the exit polls who didn't check that box a secular hedonist? As a way of explaining the outcome of the election, the "morality issue" has been amply debunked as all but meaningless.

## A "Fault Line" Running Through American Religions

But when Land uses the phrase to express his feeling of oneness with his Catholic (not to mention Jewish) brethren, it counts as a momentous development. Land does not, after all, come from some Quaker meetinghouse where all religious viewpoints are equally welcome. Rather, as the president of the Southern Baptists' Ethics and Religious Liberty Commission, he comes out of a tradition that has called the papacy the "mark of the beast." (It's no coincidence that in the *Left Behind* [book] series so beloved by evangelicals, a former American cardinal serves as lackey to the Antichrist.) Yet Land is not shy about announcing now, "I've got more in common with Pope John Paul II than I do with [former presidents] Jimmy Carter or Bill Clinton." Of course, he still has theological differences with Catholics, but "these differences are *in addition to* the basics," he says. "Together we believe in the virgin-born son, who died on the cross and was resurrected on Easter Sunday—really resurrected, like the *Washington Post* could have reported it. We

60

both say all human life is sacred, that marriage is between a man and a woman, that homosexual behavior is contrary to God's will." All this is just "more relevant," he says, "than whether I'm Catholic or Protestant."

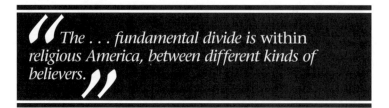

*The . . . fundamental divide is within religious America, between different kinds of believers.*

Much of the post-election commentary about the "God gap" followed the old culture-war lines drawn by [presidential candidate] Pat Buchanan at the 1992 Republican National Convention, describing this presidential race as pitting the people of God against the godless. But although that has an epic sound to it, it's wrong—if only because there are far too few godless in the country to bring [2004 Democratic presidential nominee] John Kerry to near parity. (Gallup polls show that only five percent of Americans don't believe in God or a higher power.) Rather, the election results confirmed an idea that sociologists have been dancing around [since 1995]: that the more fundamental divide is *within* religious America, between different kinds of believers. Gradually the nation's spiritual map is being redrawn into two large blocs called traditionalist and modern—or orthodox and progressive, or rejectionist and accommodationist, or some other pair of labels that academics have yet to dream up.

For most of American history, of course, the important religious divides were between denominations—not just between Protestants and Catholics and Jews but between Lutherans and Episcopalians and Southern Baptists and the other endlessly fine-tuned sects. But since the 1970s fundamental disagreements have emerged within virtually all these denominations—over abortion, over gay rights, over modernity and religion's role in it. "There's a fault line running through American religions," Land says. "And that fault line is running not between denominations but through them."

Evidence for Land's claim pops up in newspapers every year starting around springtime, when many denominations hold their biennial or quadrennial meetings. In the past the subject of contention was typically abortion; of late it's more likely to have been homosexuality. The story line is remarkably consistent. A gay minister has been ordained, or a group of bishops have blessed a gay union. An internal trial is held, and sanctions are handed out. At the denomination meeting liberal protesters wearing rainbow stoles light candles; a conservative group called Solid Rock or First Principles threatens to break away and start a splinter faction unless the denomination holds fast to tradition. A vote is taken, and the denomination barely avoids schism. Last year [2004] the Episcopal Church got the most-dramatic headlines, after an openly gay bishop was ordained in New Hampshire and a coalition of congregations broke off from the American church. But similar rifts have appeared in the past few years within the United Methodists, the Presbyterians, the Lutherans—almost any denomination one can name. Nor is it just the mainline Protestant churches. At their June [2004] meeting the American Catholic bishops split over how strictly to hold politicians accountable for their positions on abortion. When Reform rabbis sanctioned gay unions, in 2000, Conservative and Orthodox rabbis issued statements objecting. And last year [2004] the Southern Baptists voted to pull out of the Baptist World Alliance, citing a move toward liberalism that includes tolerance of homosexuality and women clergy. The proximate cause was the acceptance into the alliance of a more liberal evangelical group, the Cooperative Baptists.

## Traditionalists, Centrists, and Modernists

Every four years since 1992 a group of political scientists sponsored by the Pew Forum on Religion and Public Life has attempted to track these shifting loyalties; with each survey, says John C. Green, a professor of political science at the University of Akron and a member of the group, "the argument for the culture war in religion gets more convincing." The survey subdivides the three largest religious groups—evangelicals, mainstream Protestants, and Catholics—into "traditionalists," "centrists," and "modernists." Traditionalists are defined as having a "high view of the authority of the Bible" and worshiping regularly; they say they want to preserve "traditional beliefs and practices in a changing world." Centrists are defined as wanting to adapt beliefs to new times, while modernists have unabashedly heterodox beliefs, worship infrequently, and support upending traditional doctrines to reflect a modern view. The three categories are similar in size (centrists are a little larger and modernists a little smaller) and have remained about the same size over the dozen years of the survey.

On a wide range of issues, traditionalists agree with one another across denominations while strongly disagreeing with modernists in their own religion. For example, 32 percent of traditionalist evangelicals and 26 percent of traditionalist Catholics say abortion should always be illegal, compared with only seven percent of modernist evangelicals and three percent of modernist Catholics.

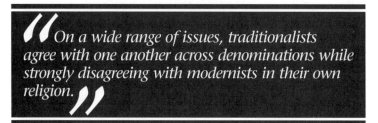

*On a wide range of issues, traditionalists agree with one another across denominations while strongly disagreeing with modernists in their own religion.*

The current divide first became apparent in the 1970s, when evangelicals, who had largely retreated from public life following the *Scopes* trial of 1925, re-engaged after *Roe v. Wade*.[1] "As the issues heated up, each side began organizing around them; then candidates picked up on them," Green says. Soon the religious landscape seemed like a copy of the political one.

Perhaps the survey's most surprising finding is the degree to which evangelicals are splintering along the same lines as all other denominations. About half the evangelicals surveyed in 2004 defined themselves as centrist or modernist. This reflects a new movement of what are sometimes called "freestyle evangelicals." They are often married women with children who attend one of those suburban megachurches where the doctrine is traditional but the style is modern. Their morals are conservative but their politics are more heterodox, featuring considerable support for education and the environment. In time they may erode the stereotype of evangelicals as overwhelmingly conservative.

The divide between traditionalists and modernists is likely to widen in the coming years. In a recent study of twenty- to thirty-four-year-olds Robert Wuthnow, the head of the Center for the Study of Religion at Princeton University, found that ide-

1. In *Scopes* the Court upheld a law that banned the teaching of evolution in schools. *Roe v. Wade* legalized abortion.

ological splits were much more pronounced than they had been in a similar study he conducted in the mid-1970s. In particular he found that political and religious views were tracking more closely, with the most religious more avidly pro-life, and the spiritual but less traditionally religious more avidly pro-choice.

Even some who are skeptical of an American "culture war" concede that religious traditionalists are gelling into a united force. According to Alan Wolfe, the author of *One Nation, After All* (1998), "The theological differences between conservative Catholics and Protestants that created five hundred years of conflict and violence have been superseded by political agreement. They are simply not interested in citing theology so long as they agree on abortion. People like Wuthnow are saying this has been going on for fifteen, twenty years. But there's an intensity this time around, much more so than most of us were prepared for."

## The Traditionalists and the Republicans

That intensity was not entirely spontaneous. From his first month in office President [George W.] Bush focused on the emerging religious split and exploited it, systematically courting traditionalist religious leaders—not only the usual Republican checklist of evangelicals but also conservative Catholic bishops and Orthodox rabbis.

According to the *National Catholic Reporter*, last year [2004] Bush asked Vatican officials for help enlisting American bishops' support on conservative issues. He held regular conference calls with Catholic conservatives, and hired Catholics to turn out the vote in their communities. He created an atmosphere that enabled a small group of outspoken leaders—including Archbishop Charles Chaput of Denver, Archbishop John Myers of Newark, Archbishop Raymond Burke of St. Louis, Bishop Michael Sheridan of Colorado Springs, and Bishop Paul Loverde of Arlington, Virginia—to make their case that public positions can't be separated from private faith.

Chaput in particular has emerged as a strong advocate of a politically engaged Catholicism. A sixty-year-old Native American, he has written stinging columns in the diocesan newsletter and an op-ed for the *New York Times* arguing that "if we believe in the sanctity of life . . . we need to prove that by our actions, including our political choices." A few weeks after the election he described his position to me at the U.S. Conference of Catholic Bishops, in Washington, D.C. As a bishop, he said, he couldn't be partisan. "We are not telling [parishioners] how to vote," he explained. "We are telling them how to take communion in good conscience." In practice that distinction can be a little hard to discern. Although in the run-up to the election Chaput never told his audiences to vote against John Kerry, he did argue that the killing of the unborn was a "nonnegotiable" issue, and then reminded them that Kerry supports abortion rights and Bush doesn't.

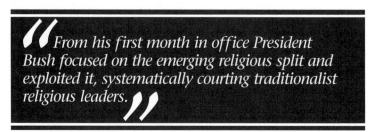

*From his first month in office President Bush focused on the emerging religious split and exploited it, systematically courting traditionalist religious leaders.*

"We've tried one approach for thirty years—to be against abortion but measured and contextualized," he explained to me. "But it hasn't rooted out abortion." Chaput says he doesn't spend much time thinking about what his position means for politics. "We're not with the Republican Party," he told the *New York Times*. "They're with us."

A still more surprising alliance seems to have arisen in the past few years between the Bush administration and the normally insular Orthodox Jewish community. Here, too, the administration's outreach has been aggressive. Bush has held Hanukkah parties at the White House with invitation lists heavy on actual rabbis—Orthodox rabbis in particular—rather than on leaders of Jewish interest groups. In 2002 the Seattle Hebrew Academy, destroyed in an earthquake, was denied federal relief funds because it was a religious institution. Soon after, Bush signed an order allowing such institutions to compete for federal funds. That year the Union of Orthodox Jewish Congregations, the largest umbrella group for Orthodox Jews, began signing on with the Southern Baptist Convention and the Christian Legal Society to support some of the administration's faith-based initiatives.

Bush closed the deal during the Republican convention last summer [2004], with an event at the Waldorf-Astoria tailored especially to Orthodox Jews—the first such event ever held by a presidential campaign. Rabbis came in from all over the country. Senator Sam Brownback, of Kansas, and Tim Goeglein, from the White House, spoke about their commitment to Israel and values. Tevi Troy, a campaign official and an Orthodox Jew, also spoke. "That event generated a lot of buzz in the Orthodox community," recalls Nathan Diament, a spokesman for the Union of Orthodox Jewish Congregations of America. "In the more insular segments of the community they don't watch TV, or get a newspaper outside the Orthodox papers. Suddenly there were headlines in the Jewish press saying the Bush campaign did this unprecedented thing, that for the first time they weren't lumping us in with the rest of the Jewish community."

The gambit worked. Thanks to Bush's attention (and, no doubt, his strong support of Israel), Hasidic enclaves—Kiryas Joel, north of Westchester [New York]; Lakewood, New Jersey; the Wickliffe suburb of Cleveland [Ohio]—voted as much as 95 percent for Bush, according to Diament, even though they had supported [Democratic candidate] Al Gore by overwhelming percentages in 2000. (The enormous swings reflect voters' loyalty to the dictates of their rabbis.) Similarly, the Miami precinct with the largest Conservative synagogue voted 80 percent for Gore in 2000 and 57 percent for Bush this time around. A strong majority of Jews nationwide voted for Kerry, but Bush's focus on politically conservative rabbis helped increase his share of the Jewish vote from 19 percent in 2000 to 25 percent last year.

"We're starting to get an echo in our community of the divide Christians have, between traditionalists and progressives," Diament says. "We do, however, have a different theology than evangelical Christians, and that theology can lead to different positions on matters of public policy." For example, Orthodox Jews don't view "an embryo sitting in a petri dish" as having the same rights as a full human being, and the Jewish imperative to heal the sick puts them in favor of stem-cell research. But, Diament says, his community shares a general sense of the corruptive influence of the mainstream culture and appreciates "the role faith plays in Bush's life and the life of his community, and how he talks about it."

## The Future of America's Religious Divide

What does the country's religious divide mean for the future? Much depends on how modernists respond to the surge of activism on the traditionalist side. If religious America is truly undergoing a culture war, it is at the moment a lopsided one.

"There's a sense of complete reversal from the late fifties and early sixties," says James Davison Hunter, the author of *Culture Wars: The Struggle to Define America* (1991). "Conservatives within denominations are so well mobilized, while progressives within Protestantism and Catholicism find themselves flat-footed, without any coherent course of action or any way to make sense of what's going on." Typically, Hunter says, evangelicals are wary of mainstream society, and prone to doomsday predictions. But he found them brimming with a "stunning sense of optimism" when he recently visited an evangelical church in Houston [Texas]. "Their understanding of their own hopes and dreams about the culture were entirely linked to getting out the vote for Bush. They seemed very pragmatic, very pleased."

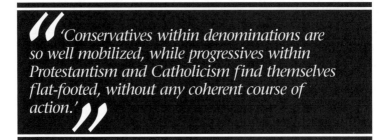

'Conservatives within denominations are so well mobilized, while progressives within Protestantism and Catholicism find themselves flat-footed, without any coherent course of action.'

For the moment, at least. It's an open question whether religious traditionalists will maintain the level of political engagement they showed in the 2004 election. The greatest obstacle here may be not a modernist backlash but the burden of high expectations. Already there are signs that evangelicals may be headed for a crushing disappointment. Following Bush's victory, James Dobson, of the evangelical group Focus on the Family, declared that if the Republicans don't deliver on issues such as abortion and gay marriage, "I believe they'll pay a price in the next election." Similarly, Bob Jones III, the president of Bob Jones University, read an open letter to Bush in chapel: "In your re-election, God has graciously granted America—though she doesn't deserve it—a reprieve from the agenda of paganism. You have been given a mandate . . . Don't equivocate. Put your agenda on the front burner and let it boil . . . Honor the Lord, and He will honor you."

It's not hard to imagine that perhaps six months, or a year, or three years down the road, religious traditionalists will face frustration and a sense of betrayal by the political system with which they are now engaging so enthusiastically. It wouldn't be the first time. After the election the conservative luminary Paul Weyrich issued a letter to evangelicals exulting, "God is indeed a Republican. He must be. His hand helped re-elect a president, with a popular mandate." And yet only five years ago [in 1999] Weyrich, who in the 1970s helped found the Heritage Foundation and coined the phrase "Moral Majority," was disillusioned about conservative Christians' ability to influence the national agenda on abortion and other issues. "Politics has failed," he wrote then. His prescription at the time: "Drop out of this culture" and find places "where we can live godly, righteous and sober lives." In 2008 we'll see if Weyrich and other religious conservatives remain engaged or start dropping out again.

# 10

# The Democratic Party Should Appeal to Religious Voters

## Michael Lerner

*Michael Lerner is a rabbi, the editor of* Tikkun *magazine, and the author of* The Politics of Meaning: Restoring Hope and Possibility in an Age of Cynicism.

The Democratic Party has been losing political ground to the Republicans because the Right is better able to engage religious voters. Republicans have championed issues that right-wing religious voters care about, but Democrats have not similarly reached out to left-wing religious voters. If the Democrats embraced religion and explained their social and foreign agendas in moral terms, they would be better able to win the support of voters.

For years the Democrats have been telling themselves "it's the economy, stupid." Yet consistently for dozens of years millions of middle-income Americans have voted against their economic interests to support Republicans who have tapped a deeper set of needs.

## Politics of Meaning

Tens of millions of Americans feel betrayed by a society that seems to place materialism and selfishness above moral values. They know that "looking out for number one" has become the common sense of our society, but they want a life that is about something more—a framework of meaning and purpose to their lives that would transcend the grasping and narcissism that surrounds them. Sure, they will admit that they have material needs, and that they worry about adequate health care, stability in employment, and enough money to give their kids a college education. But even more deeply they want their lives to have meaning—and they respond to candidates who seem to care about values and some sense of transcendent purpose.

Many of these voters have found a "politics of meaning" in the political Right. In the Right wing churches and synagogues these voters are presented with a coherent worldview that speaks to their "meaning needs." Most of these churches and synagogues demonstrate a high level of caring for their members, even if the flip side is a willingness to demean those on the outside. Yet what members experience directly is a level of mutual caring that they rarely find in the rest of the society. And a sense of community that is offered them nowhere else, a community that has as its central theme that life has value because it is connected to some higher meaning than one's success in the marketplace.

> *The liberal world has developed such a knee-jerk hostility to religion that it has . . . marginalized those many people on the Left who actually do have spiritual yearnings.*

It's easy to see how this hunger gets manipulated in ways that liberals find offensive and contradictory. The frantic attempts to preserve family by denying gays the right to get married, the talk about being conservatives while meanwhile supporting [President George W. Bush's] policies that accelerate the destruction of the environment and do nothing to encourage respect for God's creation or an ethos of awe and wonder to replace the ethos of turning nature into a commodity, the intense focus on preserving the powerless fetus and a culture of life without a concomitant commitment to medical research (stem cell research/HIV-AIDS), gun control and health-care reform, the claim to care about others and then deny them a living wage and an ecologically sustainable environment—all this is rightly perceived by liberals as a level of inconsistency that makes them dismiss as hypocrites the voters who have been moving to the Right.

Yet liberals, trapped in a long-standing disdain for religion and tone-deaf to the spiritual needs that underlie the move to the Right, have been unable to engage these voters in a serious dialogue. Rightly angry at the way that some religious communities have been mired in authoritarianism, racism, sexism and homophobia, the liberal world has developed such a knee-jerk hostility to religion that it has both marginalized those many people on the Left who actually do have spiritual yearnings and simultaneously refused to acknowledge that many who move to the Right have legitimate complaints about the ethos of selfishness in American life.

## Imagine a Religious Left

Imagine if [2004 presidential candidate] John Kerry had been able to counter George Bush by insisting that a serious religious person would never turn his back on the suffering of the poor, that the Bible's injunction to love one's neighbor required us to provide health care for all, and that the New Testament's command to "turn the other cheek" should give us a predisposition against responding to violence with violence.

Imagine a Democratic Party that could talk about the strength that comes from love and generosity and applied that to foreign policy and homeland security.

Imagine a Democratic Party that could talk of a New Bottom Line, so that American institutions get judged efficient, rational and productive not only to the extent that they maximize money and power, but also to the extent that they maximize people's capacities to be loving and caring, ethically and ecologically sensitive, and capable of responding to the universe with awe and wonder.

Imagine a Democratic Party that could call for schools to teach gratitude, generosity, caring for others, and celebration of the wonders that daily surround us! Such a Democratic Party, continuing to embrace its agenda for economic fairness and multi-cultural inclusiveness, would have won in 2004 and can win in the future.

Please don't tell me that this is happening outside the Democratic Party in the Greens or in other leftie groups—because except for a few tiny exceptions it is not! I remember how hard I tried to get Ralph Nader to think and talk in these terms in

2000, and how little response I got substantively from the Green Party when I suggested reformulating their excessively politically correct policy orientation in ways that would speak to this spiritual consciousness. The hostility of the Left to spirituality is so deep, in fact, that when they hear us in *Tikkun* talking this way they often can't even hear what we are saying—so they systematically mis-hear it and say that we are calling for the Left to take up the politics of the Right, which is exactly the opposite of our point—speaking to spiritual needs actually leads to a more radical critique of the dynamics of corporate capitalism and corporate globalization, not to a mimicking of right-wing policies.

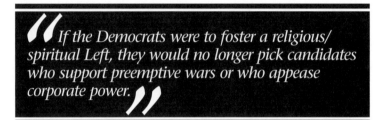

*If the Democrats were to foster a religious/ spiritual Left, they would no longer pick candidates who support preemptive wars or who appease corporate power.*

If the Democrats were to foster a religious/spiritual Left, they would no longer pick candidates who support preemptive wars or who appease corporate power. They would reject the cynical realism that led them to pretend to be born-again militarists, a deception that fooled no one and only revealed their contempt for the intelligence of most Americans. Instead of assuming that most Americans are either stupid or reactionary, a religious Left would understand that many Americans who are on the Right actually share the same concern for a world based on love and generosity that underlies Left politics, even though lefties often hide their value attachments.

## The First Step

Yet to move in this direction, many Democrats would have to give up their attachment to a core belief: that those who voted for Bush are fundamentally stupid or evil. It's time they got over that elitist self-righteousness and developed strategies that could affirm their common humanity with those who voted for the Right. Teaching themselves to see the good in the rest of the American public would be a critical first step in liberals and progressives learning how to teach the rest of American so-

72

ciety how to see that same goodness in the rest of the people on this planet. It is this spiritual lesson—that our own well-being depends on the well-being of everyone else on the planet and on the well-being of the earth—a lesson rooted deeply in the spiritual wisdom of virtually every religion on the planet, that could be the center of a revived Democratic Party.

Yet to take that seriously, the Democrats are going to have to get over the false and demeaning perception that the Americans who voted for Bush could never be moved to care about the well-being of anyone but themselves. That transformation in the Democrats would make them into serious contenders.

The last time Democrats had real social power was when they linked their legislative agenda with a spiritual politics articulated by [civil rights activist] Martin Luther King. We cannot wait for the reappearance of that kind of charismatic leader to begin the process of re-building a spiritual/religious Left.

# 11

# The Republican Party Should Stop Catering to Religious Voters

## John C. Danforth

*John C. Danforth is an Episcopal minister and a former U.S. senator from Missouri.*

The Republican Party has gone too far in advancing a conservative Christian agenda. In focusing on issues such as gay marriage and stem-cell research, Republican politicians have been advancing religious positions. By concentrating so heavily on moral issues, the Republicans have neglected issues that traditionally united their party, such as limited government, free markets and free trade, and national defense. The Republican Party should return its focus to these issues and end its fixation on the conservative Christian agenda.

Republicans have transformed our party into the political arm of conservative Christians. The elements of this transformation have included advocacy of a constitutional amendment to ban gay marriage, opposition to stem cell research involving both frozen embryos and human cells in petri dishes, and the extraordinary effort to keep Terri Schiavo [a brain-damaged woman at the center of a right-to-die dispute] hooked up to a feeding tube.

Standing alone, each of these initiatives has its advocates, within the Republican Party and beyond. But the distinct elements do not stand alone. Rather they are parts of a larger pack-

John C. Danforth, "In the Name of Politics," *The New York Times,* March 30, 2005. Copyright © 2005 by *The New York Times.* Reproduced by permission.

age, an agenda of positions common to conservative Christians and the dominant wing of the Republican Party.

## Politically Active Churches

Christian activists, eager to take credit for recent electoral successes, would not be likely to concede that Republican adoption of their political agenda is merely the natural convergence of conservative religious and political values. Correctly, they would see a causal relationship between the activism of the churches and the responsiveness of Republican politicians. In turn, pragmatic Republicans would agree that motivating Christian conservatives has contributed to their successes.

High-profile Republican efforts to prolong the life of Schiavo, including departures from Republican principles like approving congressional involvement in private decisions and empowering a federal court to overrule a state court, can rightfully be interpreted as yielding to the pressure of religious power blocs.

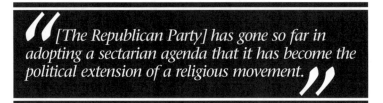

*[The Republican Party] has gone so far in adopting a sectarian agenda that it has become the political extension of a religious movement.*

In my state, Missouri, Republicans in the General Assembly have advanced legislation to criminalize even stem cell research in which the cells are artificially produced in petri dishes and will never be transplanted into the human uterus. They argue that such cells are human life that must be protected, by threat of criminal prosecution, from promising research on diseases like Alzheimer's, Parkinson's and juvenile diabetes.

It is not evident to many of us that cells in a petri dish are equivalent to identifiable people suffering from terrible diseases. I am and have always been pro-life. But the only explanation for legislators comparing cells in a petri dish to babies in the womb is the extension of religious doctrine into statutory law.

I do not fault religious people for political action. Since Moses confronted the pharaoh, faithful people have heard God's call to political involvement. Nor has political action been unique to conservative Christians. Religious liberals have been politically active in support of gay rights and against nuclear weapons and the death penalty. In America, everyone has the right to try to influence political issues, regardless of his religious motivations.

The problem is not with people or churches that are politically active. It is with a party that has gone so far in adopting a sectarian agenda that it has become the political extension of a religious movement.

## Beyond the Conservative Christian Agenda

When government becomes the means of carrying out a religious program, it raises obvious questions under the First Amendment. But even in the absence of constitutional issues, a political party should resist identification with a religious movement. While religions are free to advocate for their own sectarian causes, the work of government and those who engage in it is to hold together as one people a very diverse country. At its best, religion can be a uniting influence, but in practice, nothing is more divisive. For politicians to advance the cause of one religious group is often to oppose the cause of another.

Take stem cell research. Criminalizing the work of scientists doing such research would give strong support to one religious doctrine, and it would punish people who believe it is their religious duty to use science to heal the sick.

During the 18 years I served in the Senate, Republicans often disagreed with each other. But there was much that held us together. We believed in limited government, in keeping light the burden of taxation and regulation. We encouraged the private sector, so that a free economy might thrive. We believed that judges should interpret the law, not legislate. We were internationalists who supported an engaged foreign policy, a strong national defense and free trade. These were principles shared by virtually all Republicans.

But in recent times, we Republicans have allowed this shared agenda to become secondary to the agenda of Christian conservatives. As a senator, I worried every day about the size of the federal deficit. I did not spend a single minute worrying about the effect of gays on the institution of marriage. Today it seems to be the other way around.

The historic principles of the Republican Party offer America its best hope for a prosperous and secure future. Our current fixation on a religious agenda has turned us in the wrong direction. It is time for Republicans to rediscover our roots.

# 12

# Political Opposition to Same-Sex Marriage Is Based on Religious Beliefs

## Howard Moody

*Howard Moody is minister emeritus of Judson Memorial Church in New York City.*

The central issue in the controversy over same-sex marriage is whether religious views should form the basis of government policy. Opponents of same-sex marriage argue that the government should define marriage as being between one man and one woman, in accordance with Judeo-Christian tradition. This argument is flawed for two reasons. First, the definition of marriage has been changing for centuries, even within the Judeo-Christian tradition. Second, tying civil law to ecclesiastical law violates the principle of separation of church and state. The government should not be constrained by religious views and should recognize the right of homosexuals to marry.

If members of the church that I served for more than three decades were told I would be writing an article in defense of marriage, they wouldn't believe it. My reputation was that when people came to me for counsel about getting married, I tried to talk them out of it. More about that later.

We are now in the midst of a national debate on the nature

Howard Moody, "Gay Marriage Shows Why We Need to Separate Church and State," *Nation*, vol. 279, July 5, 2004, p. 28. Copyright © 2004 by The Nation Magazine/The Nation Company, Inc. Reproduced by permission.

of marriage, and it promises to be as emotional and polemical as the issues of abortion and homosexuality have been over the past century. What all these debates have in common is that they involved both the laws of the state and the theology of the church. The purpose of this writing is to suggest that the gay-marriage debate is less about the legitimacy of the loving relationship of a same-sex couple than about the relationship of church and state and how they define marriage.

## Multiple Traditions

In Western civilization, the faith and beliefs of Christendom played a major role in shaping the laws regarding social relations and moral behavior. Having been nurtured in the Christian faith from childhood and having served a lifetime as an ordained Baptist minister, I feel obligated first to address the religious controversy concerning the nature of marriage. If we look at the history of religious institutions regarding marriage we will find not much unanimity but amazing diversity—it is really a mixed bag. Those who base their position on "tradition" or "what the Bible says" will find anything but clarity. It depends on which "tradition" in what age reading from whose holy scriptures.

> *The gay-marriage debate is less about the legitimacy of the loving relationship of a same-sex couple than about the relationship of church and state and how they define marriage.*

In the early tradition of the Jewish people, there were multiple wives and not all of them equal. Remember the story of Abraham's wives, Sara and Hagar. Sara couldn't get pregnant, so Hagar presented Abraham with a son. When Sara got angry with Hagar, she forced Abraham to send Hagar and her son Ishmael into the wilderness. In case Christians feel superior about their "tradition" of marriage, I would remind them that their scriptural basis is not as clear about marriage as we might hope. We have Saint Paul's conflicting and condescending words about the institution: "It's better not to marry." Karl Barth called this passage the Magna Carta of the single person.

(Maybe we should have taken Saint Paul's advice more seriously. It might have prevented an earlier generation of parents from harassing, cajoling and prodding our young until they were married.) In certain religious branches, the church doesn't recognize the licensed legality of marriage but requires that persons meet certain religious qualifications before the marriage is recognized by the church. For members of the Roman Catholic Church, a "legal divorce" and the right to remarry may not be recognized unless the first marriage has been declared null and void by a decree of the church. It is clear that there is no single religious view of marriage and that history has witnessed some monumental changes in the way "husband and wife" are seen in the relationship of marriage.

## Freedom of Choice

In my faith-based understanding, if freedom of choice means anything to individuals (male or female), it means they have several options. They can be single and celibate without being thought of as strange or psychologically unbalanced. They can be single and sexually active without being labeled loose or immoral. Women can be single with child without being thought of as unfit or inadequate. If these choices had been real options, the divorce rate may never have reached nearly 50 percent.

The other, equally significant choice for people to make is that of lifetime commitment to each other and to seal that desire in the vows of a wedding ceremony. That understanding of marriage came out of my community of faith. In my years of ministry I ran a tight ship in regard to the performance of weddings. It wasn't because I didn't believe in marriage (I've been married for sixty years and have two wonderful offspring) but rather my unease about the way marriage was used to force people to marry so they wouldn't be "living in sin."

The failure of the institution can be seen in divorce statistics. I wanted people to know how challenging the promise of those vows were and not to feel this was something they had to do. My first question in premarital counseling was, "Why do you want to get married and spoil a beautiful friendship?" That question often elicited a thoughtful and emotional answer. Though I was miserly in the number of weddings I performed, I always made exceptions when there were couples who had difficulty finding clergy who would officiate. Their difficulty was because they weren't of the same religion, or they had made marital mistakes, or what they couldn't believe. Most of them were "ecclesiastical outlaws," barred from certain sacraments in the church of their choice.

## "Religious Disobedience"

The church I served had a number of gay and lesbian couples who had been together for many years, but none of them had asked for public weddings or blessings on their relationship. (There was one commitment ceremony for a gay couple at the end of my tenure.) It was as though they didn't need a piece of paper or a ritual to symbolize their lifelong commitment. They knew if they wanted a religious ceremony, their ministers would officiate and our religious community would joyfully witness.

It was my hope that since the institution of marriage had been used to exclude and demean members of the homosexual community, our church, which was open and affirming, would create with gays and lesbians a new kind of ceremony. It would be an occasion that symbolized, between two people of the same gender, a covenant of intimacy of two people to journey together, breaking new ground in human relationships—an alternative to marriage as we have known it.

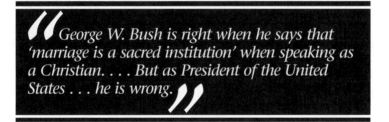

*George W. Bush is right when he says that 'marriage is a sacred institution' when speaking as a Christian. . . . But as President of the United States . . . he is wrong.*

However, I can understand why homosexuals want "to be married" in the old-fashioned "heterosexual way." After all, most gays and lesbians were born of married parents, raised in a family of siblings; many were nourished in churches and synagogues, taught about a living God before Whom all Her creatures were equally loved. Why wouldn't they conceive their loving relationships in terms of marriage and family and desire that they be confirmed and understood as such? It follows that if these gays and lesbians see their relationship as faith-based, they would want a religious ceremony that seals their intentions to become lifelong partners, lovers and friends, that they would want to be "married."

Even though most religious denominations deny this ceremony to homosexual couples, more and more clergy are, silently and publicly, officiating at religious rituals in which gays and lesbians declare their vows before God and a faith community. One Catholic priest who defied his church's ban said: "We can bless a dog, we can bless a boat, but we can't say a prayer over two people who love each other. You don't have to call it marriage, you can call it a deep and abiding friendship, but you can bless it."

We have the right to engage in "religious disobedience" to the regulations of the judicatory that granted us the privilege to officiate at wedding ceremonies, and suffer the consequences. However. when it comes to civil law, it is my contention that the church and its clergy are on much shakier ground in defying the law.

## The Government Defines Marriage

In order to fully understand the conflict that has arisen in this debate over the nature of marriage, it is important to understand the difference between the religious definition of marriage and the state's secular and civil definition. The government's interest is in a legal definition of marriage—a social and voluntary contract between a man and woman in order to protect money, property and children. Marriage is a civil union without benefit of clergy or religious definition. The state is not interested in why two people are "tying the knot," whether it's to gain money, secure a dynasty or raise children. It may be hard for those of us who have a religious or romantic view of marriage to realize that loveless marriages are not that rare. Before the [birth control] Pill, pregnancy was a frequent motive for getting married. The state doesn't care what the commitment of two people is, whether it's for life or as long as both of you love, whether it's sexually monogamous or an open marriage. There is nothing spiritual, mystical or romantic about the state's license to marry—it's a legal contract.

Thus, George W. Bush is right when he says that "marriage is a sacred institution" when speaking as a Christian, as a member of his Methodist church. But as President of the United States and leader of all Americans, believers and unbelievers, he is wrong. What will surface in this debate as litigation and court decisions multiply is the history of the conflict between the church and the state in defining the nature of marriage.

That history will become significant as we move toward a decision on who may be married.

After Christianity became the state religion of the Roman Empire in AD 325, the church maintained absolute control over the regulation of marriage for some 1,000 years. Beginning in the sixteenth century, English kings (especially Henry VIII, who found the inability to get rid of a wife extremely oppressive) and other monarchs in Europe began to wrest control from the church over marital regulations. Ever since, kings, presidents and rulers of all kinds have seen how important the control of marriage is to the regulation of social order. In this nation, the government has always been in charge of marriage. . . .

Now even though it is the civil authority of the state that defines the rights and responsibilities of marriage and therefore who can be married, the state is no more infallible than the church in its judgments. It wasn't until the mid-twentieth century that the Supreme Court declared antimiscegenation laws unconstitutional. Even after that decision, many mainline churches, where I started my ministry, unofficially discouraged interracial marriages, and many of my colleagues were forbidden to perform such weddings.

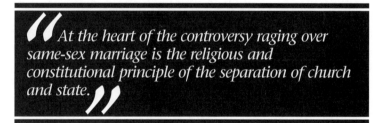

*At the heart of the controversy raging over same-sex marriage is the religious and constitutional principle of the separation of church and state.*

The civil law view of marriage has as much historical diversity as the church's own experience because, in part, the church continued to influence the civil law. Although it was the Bible that made "the husband the head of his wife," it was common law that "turned the married pair legally into one person—the husband," as Nancy Cott documents in her book *Public Vows: A History of Marriage and the Nation* (an indispensable resource for anyone seeking to understand the changing nature of marriage in the nation's history). She suggests that "the legal doctrine of marital unity was called coverture . . . [which] meant that the wife could not use legal avenues such as suits or contracts, own assets, or execute legal documents without her husband's collaboration." This view of the wife would not hold water in any court in the land today.

As a matter of fact, even in the religious understanding of President Bush and his followers, allowing same-sex couples the right to marry seems a logical conclusion. If marriage is "the most fundamental institution of civilization" and a major contributor to the social order in our society, why would anyone want to shut out homosexuals from the "glorious attributes" of this "sacred institution"? Obviously, the only reason one can discern is that the opponents believe that gay and lesbian people are not worthy of the benefits and spiritual blessings of "marriage."

## Separation of Church and State

At the heart of the controversy raging over same-sex marriage is the religious and constitutional principle of the separation of church and state. All of us can probably agree that there was never a solid wall of separation, riddled as it is with breaches. The evidence of that is seen in the ambiguity of tax-free religious institutions, "in God we trust" printed on our money and "under God" in the Pledge of Allegiance to our country. All of us clergy, who are granted permission by the state to officiate at legal marriage ceremonies, have already compromised the "solid wall" by signing the license issued by the state. I would like to believe that my authority to perform religious ceremonies does not come from the state but derives from the vows of ordination and my commitment to God. I refuse to repeat the words, "by the authority invested in me by the State of New York, I pronounce you husband and wife," but by signing the license, I've become the state's "handmaiden."

> *The definition of marriage has been changing over the centuries in this nation, and it will change yet again as homosexuals are seen as ordinary human beings.*

It seems fitting therefore that we religious folk should now seek to sharpen the difference between ecclesiastical law and civil law as we beseech the state to clarify who can be married by civil law. Further evidence that the issue of church and state is part of the gay-marriage controversy is that two Unitarian ministers have been arrested for solemnizing unions between same-sex couples when no state licenses were involved. Ecclesiastical law may punish those clergy who disobey marital regulations, but the state has no right to invade church practices and criminalize clergy under civil law. There should have been a noisy outcry from all churches, synagogues and mosques at the government's outrageous contravention of the sacred principle of the "free exercise of religion."

I come from a long line of Protestants who believe in a "free church in a free state." In the issue before this nation, the civil law is the determinant of the regulation of marriage, regardless of our religious views, and the Supreme Court will finally decide what the principle of equality means in our Constitution in the third century of our life together as a people. It is likely that the Commonwealth of Massachusetts will probably lead the nation on this matter, as the State of New York led to the Supreme Court decision to allow women reproductive freedom.

## An Evolving Institution

So what is marriage? It depends on whom you ask, in what era, in what culture. Like all words or institutions, human definitions, whether religious or secular, change with time and history. When our beloved Constitution was written, blacks, Native Americans and, to some extent, women were quasi-human beings with no rights or privileges, but today they are recognized as persons with full citizenship rights. The definition of marriage has been changing over the centuries in this nation, and it will change yet again as homosexuals are seen as ordinary human beings.

In time, and I believe that time is now, we Americans will see that all the fears foisted on us by religious zealots were not real. Heterosexual marriage will still flourish with its statistical failures. The only difference will be that some homosexual couples will join them and probably account for about the same number of failed relationships. And we will discover that it did not matter whether the couples were joined in a religious ceremony or a secular and civil occasion for the statement of their intentions.

# 13

# Political Opposition to Same-Sex Marriage Is Based on a Concern for Society

## Richard Bastien

*Richard Bastien is a writer and a representative of the Catholic Civil Rights League.*

Homosexuals who advocate same-sex marriage often argue that they are the victims of religious discrimination, contending that they are denied access to a social institution solely on the basis of other people's religious beliefs. However, marriage is defined as being between one man and one woman not simply for religious reasons, but because such a definition is best for society. The ultimate purpose of marriage is procreation, which is necessary for the continuation of society. Homosexual couples, by definition, cannot procreate. In their quest to legalize same-sex marriage, homosexuals are attacking and harming traditional culture.

Same-sex "marriage" is but the latest episode in the culture war. This becomes obvious if one analyzes the arguments supporting that concept and links them to those aspects of our modern culture that give it an aura of legitimacy. Most of the literature supporting same-sex marriage boils down to two basic arguments: the inequity of traditional marriage and the bigotry of those upholding it.

Richard Bastien, "Same-Sex Marriage and the Culture War," *Catholic Insight,* vol. 13, February 2005, pp. 30–33. Copyright © 2005 by *Catholic Insight*. Reproduced by permission.

I will depict both arguments as honestly as possible, show why they are intellectually unsustainable, and then indicate why our culture is nevertheless unable to refute their apparent legitimacy. Finally, I will propose a strategy, not of resistance, but of conquest. A conquest of hearts and souls.

## The Inequity Argument (Oxford Dictionary: Inequitable = Unfair, Unjust)

The inequity argument invoked by the homosexual lobby runs as follows: our agenda puts no restriction on whom heterosexuals can marry, but the prevailing rules impose a major one on us. Allowing us to marry would enhance our happiness without diminishing that of heterosexual couples. So long as "straights" are not forced into marrying people of their sex, why should they care about whether same-sex couples marry or not?

The argument is as clever as it is deceptive. If the definition of marriage is broadened to include gay couples, the meaning of marriage will be changed not only for gays but for all, including heterosexuals. Instead of a life covenant based on a procreative promise, it would become a mere contract between any two individuals.

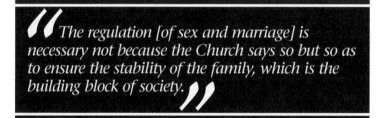

*The regulation [of sex and marriage] is necessary not because the Church says so but so as to ensure the stability of the family, which is the building block of society.*

The law recognizes marriage not only because it entails a contractual relationship between two persons, but because that contractual relationship is consistent with the good of society and the State (which also includes the good of individuals). Marriage is generally ordered to the procreation of new persons, to whose education and upbringing the spouses commit themselves. Same-sex couples are, by nature, incapable of procreation. Moreover, most of them admit to never aspiring to any life commitment (more on this later). Consequently, giving such couples the legal status and rights proper to marriage would be unjust. Those rights are linked to the expectation of duration and procreation. If there is no promise of procreation, why should the State care about marriage?

The inequity argument wrongly assumes that sexual morality has to do solely with the behaviour of individuals. It ignores its importance for family and society. Without sexual morality, the unity of the couple and of the family is shattered. And since marriage and family are part and parcel of the social order, sexual morality impacts very meaningfully on society also. This is precisely why marriage is a social institution.

Because of its strength, the human sexual impulse must be regulated. The regulation is necessary not because the Church says so but so as to ensure the stability of the family, which is the building block of society. The upshot is that, for the family to fulfill its role and for ordered liberty to exist, some constraints on sexual conduct are required. Marriage, family, and ordered liberty cannot co-exist with widespread sexual permissiveness. The more there is of the latter, the less of the former, and vice-versa. This is illustrated by the experience of Soviet Russia where, in the early twenties, Communist rulers undertook to abolish the legal registration of marriage. According to the Soviet prosecutor of the time, [Nikolai] Krilenko, the rationale for such a move was as follows:

> "Why should the State know who marries whom?
> . . . Free love is the ultimate aim of a socialist state;
> in that State marriage will be free from any kind of
> obligation, including economic, and will turn into
> an absolutely free union of two beings".

The agenda of the homosexual lobby and of radical feminists fits perfectly with that statement. Yet the Soviet experiment was a dismal failure and marriage was soon restored.

## The Homosexual Lifestyle

Concepts such as life commitment, conjugal fidelity, and social stability are completely foreign to the homosexual lifestyle. A study of homosexual men under age 30 in Amsterdam [Netherlands], sponsored by the Dutch AIDS project and published in *AIDS* 2003, found that single men acquire 22 casual partners a year, men with a steady partner acquire eight casual partners a year, and "steady partnerships" last an average of 18 months. In a book published in 1996 and entitled *Virtually Normal*, Andrew Sullivan argues that stable homosexual couples have a "need for extramarital outlets".

All this helps to understand why homosexual activists tend to view society as an amalgam of people regulated solely by the State. The notion that between the State and the individual stands another natural institution—the family—and that families develop institutions of their own, such as schools and local churches, seems totally alien to their mindset. According to their understanding of equality, whether a boy grows up to marry another boy or a girl has no social relevance. But equality does not entail the right to redefine marriage: we are all equal vis-a-vis the social institution of marriage.

## The Bigotry Argument

The other argument in support of gay marriage is that traditional marriage is grounded not in reason but in religious belief, which is assumed to be devoid of any rational content. Michael Kinsley, editor of *Slate Magazine*, put it this way in a recent column:

> "We on my side . . . don't . . . believe that our values are direct orders from God. We don't claim they are immutable and beyond argument. We are, if anything, crippled by reason and open-mindedness, by a desire to persuade rather than insist".

The argument wrongly assumes that anyone who opposes same-sex marriage is doing so solely for religious reasons and is in effect imposing his religious values on others. In other words, opposition to same-sex marriage is deemed to be rooted in bigotry. This ignores the fact that religious people who oppose gay marriage generally do so not solely on the basis of religion, but also on the basis of reason. For example, a statement issued by [Pope] John Paul II on June 3, 2003, makes the following point:

> "Homosexual unions are . . . lacking in the biological and anthropological elements . . . which would be the basis, on the level of reason, for granting them legal recognition. Such unions are not able to contribute in a proper way to the procreation and survival of the human race."

Far from being opposed, faith and reason support each other. This being said, there is a deeper flaw in the bigotry argument. It is the claim that, in these matters, only people who do not take their cue from God can truly argue in reason. People who think like the editor of *Slate* magazine, i.e. the bulk of academia and the media, think that the litmus test of "reason and open-mindedness" is complete divorce from any religious faith. This is the secular humanist view of the world, one in which there is no God, the world of the spirit does not exist, and man is a mere animal—a sophisticated chimpanzee. People who adopt this view are free to do so. However, they must realize that their choice gives them no claim to some kind of intellectual or moral superiority vis-a-vis people who profess a religious faith.

Secular humanism is itself a system of beliefs, just like Christianity, Judaism, or Islam, and no less dogmatic than the latter. For example, the Humanist Manifesto of 1933 declared that "religious humanists" believe the universe to be "self-existing and not created", that "man is a part of nature, and that he has emerged as the result of a continuous process." An updated version published in 1973 reiterates these ideas and states that "moral values derive their source from human experience."

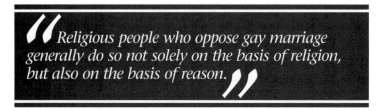

*Religious people who oppose gay marriage generally do so not solely on the basis of religion, but also on the basis of reason.*

These ideas are simply taken for granted and never proven. For humanists to claim they only are "crippled by reason and open-mindedness" is thus pure arrogance. Indeed, it is a case of religious intolerance.

Anyone who thinks this is an exaggeration should read what leading secular humanists have been saying in recent years. I recommend an article by Robert Reich, a senior member of the Clinton administration, who lately argued that

> "the great conflict of the 21st century will be between modern civilization and anti-modernists . . . between those who believe in the primacy of the individual and those who believe that human beings owe their allegiance . . . to a higher authority; . . . between those who believe in science, reason, and logic and those who believe that truth is revealed through Scripture and religious dogma."

This statement displays as much ignorance as it does arrogance. If Reich had his facts straight, he would know that many great scientists also believe in a personal God. He would also know that allegiance to a higher authority, far from diminishing respect for the individual, enhances it.

## The Broader Religious War

It would be nice to stop here and conclude that the arguments about same-sex marriage are rooted in a secular humanist tradition whose claim to intellectual and moral superiority is demonstrably unfounded. But, unfortunately, the story does not end here. What we are up against is not just phony arguments but a vast strategy of deception. The debate on marriage is part of a broader religious war. And Christians need be made aware of this lest they soon find themselves stripped of their religious rights.

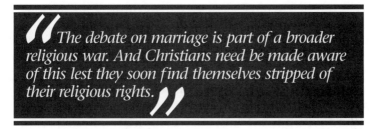

*The debate on marriage is part of a broader religious war. And Christians need be made aware of this lest they soon find themselves stripped of their religious rights.*

The issue of gay "marriage" has come about because the homosexual lobby has a strategy. In 1990, Marshall Kirk and Hunter Madsen published a book entitled *After the Ball: How America Will Conquer Its Fear and Hatred of Gays in the 90's*, setting out how the gay movement should go about achieving its objectives. In an article entitled "The Overhauling of Straight America", Kirk summarized the strategy as follows:

> {We} can undermine the moral authority of homophobic churches by portraying them as antiquated backwaters, badly out of step with the times and with the latest findings of psychology. Against the mighty pull of institutional Religion one must set the mightier draw of Science and Public Opinion. Such an unholy alliance has worked well against churches before, on such topics as divorce and abortion. . . . Our campaign should not demand direct

support for homosexual practices; but should instead take anti-discrimination as its theme.

*Myth 1.* Science and Public Opinion: these are the tools that the homosexual lobby pretends it has been using to advance its agenda. But again, that claim simply does not square with the facts. The evidence provided in support of gay marriage has been shown to be phony. For example, gay activists tried for years to propagate the idea that they represent 10 percent of the population. They invoked "scientific research" done by the great guru of the Sexual Revolution, Alfred Kinsey, to support that claim. Yet no reputable scientific survey has ever been able to duplicate Kinsey's findings. And it is now generally acknowledged that his number was widely inflated.

*Myth 2.* The other myth propagated by the homosexual lobby and the media to legitimize gay marriage is that people are born with their sexual orientation. Yet no one in the medical community subscribes to this view. How could it be otherwise? If homosexuality were genetic, evolutionary science suggests that it would have died out. A survey of the literature on this issue indicates that research has yet to find any "gay gene."

Interestingly, there is one thing that the literature does show clearly, although it is hardly ever acknowledged by the homosexual lobby or the media: many people have changed from a homosexual orientation to a heterosexual orientation with and without therapy. The complicity of silence on this matter is simply astounding.

What the foregoing suggests is that:

- arguments in support of same-sex "marriage" are intellectually unsustainable; and
- the push for same-sex "marriage" is part of a wider agenda based on junk science aimed at eradicating any remnant of Christian culture.

# 14

# Political Opposition to Stem-Cell Research Is Based on Religious Beliefs

## Robert Kuttner

*Robert Kuttner is coeditor of the* American Prospect.

Although President Bush's policy on stem-cell research was hailed as a reasonable compromise by the mainstream media, in reality the policy was designed to appease religious fundamentalists who oppose all stem-cell research. By limiting federal funding for stem-cell research while also allowing the research to continue in the private sector, Bush has been able to pay lip service to his religious constituents without really addressing the serious issues surrounding stem-cell research.

*Editor's note: Research on stem cells from human embryos could lead to groundbreaking medical advances, but many religious groups oppose it because it involves the destruction of human embryos. In August 2001 President George W. Bush limited the types of stem-cell research that may qualify for federal funding while leaving private research largely unregulated.*

President [George W.] Bush's heavily choreographed decision to support "limited" stem cell research generated the desired headlines and TV commentary. He had anguished over

Robert Kuttner, "The Great Obfuscator," *American Prospect,* vol. 12, September 10, 2001, p. 2. Copyright © 2001 by The American Prospect, Inc. All rights reserved. Reproduced with permission from *American Prospect*, 11 Beacon Street, Suite 1120, Boston, MA 02108.

the decision, we were told, and navigated a prudent course between zealous scientists who would play God and zealous traditionalists who claim a pipeline to God. Under Bush's guidelines, stem cell research can qualify for federal funding if it involves existing "lines" of privately developed embryonic stem cells. Others could not, but the harvesting of stem cells from human embryos can continue with private funding. Bush had carefully chosen a middle ground between, as he put it, the good and the good.

This construct is, of course, nonsense. Bush has essentially let science policy be dictated by fundamentalist Protestant views about when life begins. (The Catholic hierarchy, which consistently opposes trifling with embryos under whatever auspices, lent cover to Bush's middle-ground charade by helpfully opposing his policy.)

## An Incoherent Policy

The policy is anything but coherent, either as ethics or as science. If harvesting of embryonic stem cells is morally dubious, why should it be prohibited with federal funding but allowed in private laboratories? And why should new colonies of stem cells be suspect but existing ones be acceptable? Bush's spurious distinction recalls thousands of years of cynically corrupt theological expediency—sales of indulgences, deals between popes and kings—and it reminds us why preachers should be kept far away from the laboratory to begin with.

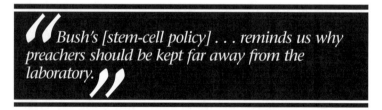

*Bush's [stem-cell policy] . . . reminds us why preachers should be kept far away from the laboratory.*

Let's not forget: Though he has obfuscated his position and winked at the religious right, Bush declined the opportunity to say that a woman should be denied the right to terminate a pregnancy. So if an embryo can be destroyed at will for no specified reason, why on earth object to destroying embryos in the course of scientific research?

There are plenty of ethical questions to address, but Bush ducked them. Should we use surplus embryos discarded from fertility clinics but not those created explicitly for their stem cells? Should we breed embryonic clones for spare parts for a particular individual? What about whole-human clones? But this is not the moral realm Bush inhabits. His policy simply allows private industry to continue developing embryos willy-nilly—activity that Bush considers too morally suspect to get public funds. How touchingly Republican that Bush would give corporate industry an indulgence that he denies to socially funded activity. If the market does it, then by definition it must be okay.

> *We need to see Bush's policy for what it is—a pure sop to the fundamentalist right.*

Bush's approach sidesteps and thereby aggravates a more serious threat to biomedical progress. The real question is: Which scientific advances shall be publicly funded, publicly regulated, and left in the public domain, and which shall be private and proprietary? This issue—and not the theological questions about when embryonic life begins—is the truly difficult policy question crying out for resolution.

## Pandering to the Religious Right

By disdaining public science in favor of pandering to the religious right, Bush tacitly resolves the question in favor of the private biotech industry. In effect, the religious right is a stalking horse for companies like Geron, which no longer need to fear competition from the National Institutes of Health. After all, if most funding must proceed privately, then the government will have little leverage over who shall gain access to the products of the research and on what terms. Private stem cell colonies will be available only based on licenses from the patent holder. Scientists at the University of Wisconsin, which has a lucrative deal with Geron, are now suing their university to pursue access to the research products.

As science policy, Bush's approach makes stem cell research a more extreme version of the path taken by pharmaceutical research. Instead of broad access and collaboration in the scientific community, stem cell breakthroughs will be proprietary products. So when the miracle cures come, they will be available only at astronomical costs to a narrow public, the science will be needlessly balkanized, and the Medicare budget will take another beating. When Bush announced his policy, most scientists were aghast, but executives of Geron were cheering.

In a stroke, Bush has managed to alienate many religious conservatives as well as most scientists. But that hardly means that his policy adds up to a sensible middle ground. One way or another, this use of embryonic stem cells will continue—if not in the United States, then overseas. And if the right persists with efforts to ban such research outright, it will only drive stem cell research offshore all the faster, to the detriment of U.S. science.

Though Bush did it pretty effectively in the campaign, it's hard to obfuscate the issue of reproductive choice. One either favors restricting a woman's right to choose or does not. But the issue of human-embryo cloning and science policy is much easier to fuzz up, because there are genuinely difficult policy questions involving moral quandaries and subtle issues of intellectual-property law as well as public science versus proprietary science. And these questions come bundled with technical concepts that few lay people easily grasp.

We need to see Bush's policy for what it is—a pure sop to the fundamentalist right. This republic, with its legions of true believers, has done best when it followed [Thomas] Jefferson's strict separation of private belief and public business. Bush's stoking of the fundamentalist brimstone with his "faith-based" and "pro-life" pandering is pure mischief. It's bad enough to allow a fanatic minority to dictate its views on reproductive rights. It's even worse to let private religious dogmas restrict research that could relieve suffering, enrich health, and extend life.

# 15

# Political Opposition to Stem-Cell Research Is Based on Respect for Human Life

Jacqueline Lee

*Jacqueline Lee is a freelance writer.*

Embryonic stem-cell research is a morally complex issue for many people. On the one hand, the research has the potential to cure many fatal diseases. On the other hand, it involves the destruction of human embryos. Because all human beings begin as embryos, logic dictates that embryos are alive and are human. No matter what the benefits of embryonic stem-cell research may be, it is unethical to create or purposely destroy embryos for medical research. To do so is to violate the Nuremberg Code, a secular treaty that governs scientific research on humans. Clearly, objections to embryonic stem-cell research are not strictly religious in nature but are secular as well.

Watching someone you love turn to stone before your eyes can definitely affect your perspective on the embryonic stem-cell research debate. In 1999, my mother was diagnosed with scleroderma, which literally means hard skin. For a person with this rare disease, the immune system, which is supposed to attack the pathogens that make us ill, turns instead on

Jacqueline Lee, "Embryonic Stem Cells: The End Doesn't Justify the Means," *U.S. Catholic*, vol. 67, January 2002, p. 24. Copyright © 2002 by *U.S. Catholic*. Reproduced by permission. Subscriptions: $22/year from 205 West Monroe, Chicago, IL 60606; Call 1-800-328-6515 for subscription information or visit www.us catholic.org.

healthy body tissues. Symptoms may begin with tightening and thickening of the skin along with joint and muscle pain. Patients may then develop Raynaud's phenomenon, a condition in which the body's extremities change color in response to temperature. Others may develop calcinosis, white lumps beneath the skin that can erupt, leaving painful ulcers.

My mother's first symptom was shortness of breath. The disease viciously attacked her lungs and other internal organs, and she died of respiratory failure within seven months of her diagnosis. During that time, she lost the ability to get up from a sitting position without assistance. She lost 50 pounds because she could not eat anything without vomiting. She lost her ability to breathe. In the end, instead of praying for her recovery, I began to pray that she would be released from her struggle with the disease. As soon as she died, I begged God for the chance to take that prayer back.

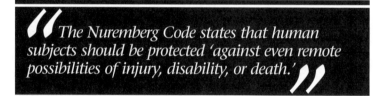

*The Nuremberg Code states that human subjects should be protected 'against even remote possibilities of injury, disability, or death.'*

According to research presented last year [2001] by University of Florida professor of medicine John R. Wingard, stem-cell transplants show remarkable promise in treating not only scleroderma but also other autoimmune diseases like multiple sclerosis and lupus. Essentially, stem cells are the body's "master cells." They can differentiate into other types of cells, from brain cells to skin cells. Feasibly, stem cells might be injected into the nervous system to replace tissues damaged by strokes, Alzheimer's, Parkinson's, or spinal cord injuries.

I am excited about the potential of stem-cell therapies, but recent demands that the federal government fund research on embryonic stem cells frighten me. Extracting stem cells from embryos proves contentious, of course, because embryos must be destroyed in order to obtain the cells.

## Embryonic vs. Adult Stem-Cell Research

Supporters of embryonic stem-cell research cite two main advantages of embryonic stem cells—both of them, ultimately, economic. According to the National Institutes of Health, stem cells from embryos, so-called "pluripotent" cells, are more flexible than adult stem cells and can thus be manipulated into more types of body tissues, including bone, skin, and muscle. Those who support federal funding of embryonic stem-cell research claim that pluripotent cells are more useful than adult stem cells because they possess these remarkable powers of transformation. In addition, scientists can generate an unlimited number of embryonic stem cells in the laboratory. Because adult cells are more difficult to obtain, embryos would be a more cost-effective source of cells.

"We are now witnessing the gradual restructuring of American culture according to ideals of utility, productivity, and cost-effectiveness," wrote the U.S. Catholic bishops in *Living the Gospel of Life: A Challenge to American Catholics.* "It is a culture where moral questions are submerged by a river of goods and services."

But opponents of embryonic research, ironically, are able to cite the economic argument, too. According to [an] article by Scott Gottlieb in the *American Spectator,* investors of venture capital currently fund adult stem-cell research much more frequently than they fund embryonic research. Why? Embryonic cells have never been used in humans, but adult cells have.

Opponents also note that embryonic cells can, at times, be too flexible. Gottlieb notes that the injection of pluripotent cells in mice, for instance, has caused the growth of tumors consisting of numerous body tissue types; the cells did not integrate themselves into damaged tissues as scientists hoped they would. Also, conceivably, a transplanted embryonic stem cell could be rejected by the recipient's body—much like the body tries to reject a transplanted organ. Adult stem cells, however, are more specialized and, because adult stem cells are harvested from the patient's own body, rejection is not a factor.

## The Destruction of Human Life Is Immoral

Apart from medical and economic arguments, we as Catholics must wade through the ambiguous moral arguments both for and against embryonic research. While many prolife Catholic organizations, including the National Catholic Bioethics Center, have staunchly opposed stem-cell research, according to a *Wall Street Journal*/NBC News Poll, a majority of Catholics surveyed—72 percent—support it.

Senator Orrin Hatch of Utah, a leading supporter of embryonic research, argues that "a frozen embryo in a refrigerator in a clinic" is not the same as "a fetus developing in a mother's womb." These frozen embryos, his supporters say, have the potential to develop into life—but the embryos themselves are not technically alive.

Many bioethicists, however, dismiss that argument as pointless rationalization. If all humans begin as embryos, how can embryos not be considered "alive"? Furthermore, if these embryos are alive, then extracting embryonic stem cells violates at least three principles of the Nuremberg Code, which lays out principles scientists must observe when conducting research on human subjects. First, scientists must always obtain the voluntary consent of every human research subject. Embryos, of course, cannot give their consent. Also, when scientists create embryos specifically for the purposes of experimentation, the embryos do not even have parents who can speak on their behalf.

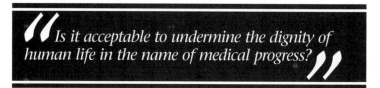

*Is it acceptable to undermine the dignity of human life in the name of medical progress?*

Second, the Nuremberg Code states that human subjects should be protected "against even remote possibilities of injury, disability, or death." Third, the Nuremberg Code requires that experiments on human subjects must yield results "unprocurable by any other means of study."

If experimental treatments involving adult cells have already furnished promising results, why do we need embryonic cells? And if embryonic research violates the codes we have established to protect human dignity, how can we, as moral people, even consider carrying it out?

As Tommy Thompson, U.S. Secretary of Health and Human Services—and a prominent Catholic—observes, "There is nothing easy about this issue. It balances our respect for human life with our highest hopes for alleviating human suffering." True, pluripotent cells in and of themselves cannot develop into human beings. However, scientists cannot obtain pluripotent cells without destroying the four-day-old embryos from which they come. "As long as embryos are destroyed as part of the research enterprise," says the National Bioethics Advisory Council, "researchers using embryonic stem cells (and those who fund them) will be complicit in the death of embryos."

With his decision in August [2001], President [George W.] Bush has already authorized limited funding for research on existing stem-cell lines. . . . Although many respect Bush's compromise, my own fear is that his willingness to allow a little funding has paved the way for steady relaxation of current restrictions.

## The Ends Cannot Justify the Means

Ultimately, it comes down to this: Can we really justify the willful destruction of human embryos by arguing that "the end justifies the means"? Is it acceptable to undermine the dignity of human life in the name of medical progress?

Perhaps many of us are looking at this issue through swollen eyes blurred by tears. We have all seen the suffering brought on by degenerative illness, either in ourselves or in someone we love. Our hearts ache for those who suffer, and we want to do anything by any means to stop it.

But, no matter how laudable that aim may be, it cannot justify the destruction of a developing human life. In the words of Charlotte Brontë's *Jane Eyre*, "Law and principles are not for times when there is no temptation: They are for such moments as this, when body and soul rise in mutiny against their rigor. If at my individual convenience I might break them, what would be their worth?"

My heart ached for my mother, and today it aches for all those who suffer from disease and injury; but, no matter how deep my desire to ease that suffering may be, it cannot justify the destruction of a developing human life. I wish that my mother had been strong enough to undergo a stem-cell transplant. I would have done anything to save her.

Well, almost anything. I would not have been complicit in the destruction of human life, even if the destruction of that life could have saved hers. To me, a praiseworthy end could never have justified such a destructive means.

# Organizations to Contact

**American Atheists**
PO Box 5733, Parsippany, NJ 07054-6733
(908) 276-7300 • fax: (908) 276-7402
e-mail: info@atheists.org • Web site: www.aetheists.org

American Atheists is a nationwide movement that defends the civil rights of nonbelievers, works for the separation of church and state, and addresses issues of First Amendment public policy. It publishes the *Atheist Viewpoint* as well as *AANEWS*, an e-mail newsletter.

**American Civil Liberties Union (ACLU)**
125 Broad St., Eighteenth Fl., New York, NY 10004
Web site: www.aclu.org

The ACLU is a national organization that defends Americans' civil rights guaranteed in the U.S. Constitution, including the separation of church and state and the right to practice one's religion free of government interference. The ACLU opposes government funding for faith-based organizations and religious displays on government property. It publishes numerous materials, including news alerts about church and state developments, on its Web site.

**American Enterprise Institute (AEI)**
1150 Seventeenth St. NW, Washington, DC 20036
(202) 862-5800 • fax: (202) 862-7177
Web site: www.aei.org

AEI is a think tank dedicated to preserving and strengthening conservative values such as limited government, private enterprise, and freedom of religion through scholarly research, open debate, and publications. The institute publishes dozens of books and hundreds of articles and reports each year, as well as the policy magazine *American Enterprise*. Articles available on the AEI Web site include "Freedom of Religion Versus Freedom from Religion," "The Faith of the Founding," and "Are We a Nation 'Under God'?"

**Americans for Religious Liberty (ARL)**
PO Box 6656, Silver Spring, MD 20916
(301) 260-2988 • fax: (301) 260-2989
e-mail: info@arlinc.org • Web site: www.arlinc.org

ARL promotes and defends the separation of church and state through publishing, research, litigation, coalition building, public speaking, and expert testimony before national and state legislative committees. It opposes the display of religious symbols on government property and government funding for faith-based social service organizations and religious schools. ARL publishes a newsletter and a variety of books on church-state separation.

## Americans United for Separation of Church and State
518 C St. NE, Washington, DC 20002
(202) 466-3234
e-mail: americansunited@au.org • Web site: www.au.org

Americans United for Separation of Church and State is a nonprofit organization that works to defend religious freedom by advocating church-state separation and opposing measures such as mandatory prayer in public schools, tax dollars for parochial schools, and involvement in partisan politics by religious groups. The organization litigates in court cases pertaining to church-state separation. It publishes *Church & State* magazine.

## Brookings Institution
1775 Massachusetts Ave. NW, Washington, DC 20036
(202) 797-6000 • fax: (202) 797-6004
Web site: www.brook.edu

The institution is an independent, nonpartisan organization devoted to research, analysis, and public education with an emphasis on economics, foreign policy, governance, and metropolitan policy. The Religion & Civil Society project, part of Brookings's Governance Studies program, examines the role of religion in citizenship, community and national service, and government policy-making. The institute publishes books such as *One Electorate Under God?: A Dialogue on Religion and American Politics*, and the project Web site features analysis, commentary, and transcripts from debates and symposiums.

## Call to Renewal
2401 Fifteenth St. NW, Washington DC 20009
(202) 328-8745 • fax: (202) 328-6797
e-mail: ctr@calltorenewal.org • Web site: www.calltorenewal.org

Call to Renewal is a national network of Christian churches, faith-based organizations, and individuals working to overcome poverty in America. It works to influence local and national public policies and priorities while growing and developing a movement of Christians committed to overcoming poverty. It publishes *The Call*, an e-infoletter.

## Council for Secular Humanism
PO Box 664, Amherst, NY 14226-0664
(716) 636-7571 • fax: (716) 636-1733
e-mail: info@secularhumanism.org
Web site: www.secularhumanism.org

The council cultivates rational inquiry, ethical values, and human development through the advancement of secular humanism. It sponsors publications and programs, and it organizes meetings and other group activities to serve the needs of nonreligious people. The council publishes the magazine *Free Inquiry* and the newsletter *Secular Humanist Bulletin*.

### Family Research Council (FRC)
8801 G. St. NW, Washington, DC 20001
(202) 393-2100 • fax: (202) 393-2134
Web site: www.frc.org

The council champions marriage and family as the foundation of civilization and promotes the Judeo-Christian worldview as the basis for a just, free, and stable society. FRC shapes public debate and formulates public policy that values human life and upholds the institutions of marriage and the family. It publishes hundreds of reports, fact sheets, and opinion pieces on these issues.

### Focus on the Family
8605 Explorer Dr., Colorado Springs, CO 80995
(800) 232-6459
Web site: www.family.org

Focus on the Family is an evangelical Christian organization that seeks to preserve traditional values and the institution of the family. The organization opposes abortion, embryonic stem-cell research, and same-sex marriage and supports the free exercise of religion and the right of religious persons to participate in political debate. It publishes *Citizen* magazine and provides many news alerts and commentaries on its Web site.

### Interfaith Alliance
1331 H St. NW, Eleventh Fl., Washington, DC 20005
(800) 510-0969 • fax: (202) 639-6375
e-mail: info@interfaithalliance.org
Web site: www.interfaithalliance.org

The alliance is a group of religious leaders who work to promote interfaith cooperation around shared religious values to strengthen the public's commitment to the American values of civic participation, freedom of religion, diversity, and civility in public discourse. The organization encourages the active involvement of people of faith in the nation's political life. It publishes a quarterly newsletter called the *Light* and *Media Roundup*, a summary of news stories where religion—either positively or negatively—has played a role in a political candidate's quest for elected office.

### Pew Forum on Religion & Public Life
1615 L St. NW, Suite 700, Washington, DC 20036-5610
(202) 419-4550 • fax: (202) 419-4559
e-mail: info@pewforum.org • Web site: http://pewforum.org

The Pew Forum on Religion & Public Life seeks to promote a deeper understanding of issues at the intersection of religion and public affairs. As a nonpartisan, nonadvocacy organization, the forum does not take positions on policy debates, but instead pursues its mission by delivering timely, impartial information to national opinion leaders, including government officials and journalists. It publishes surveys such as "The American Religious Landscape and the 2004 Presidential Vote: Increased Polarization" and reports such as *A Faith-Based Partisan Divide*.

**Pluralism Project**
1531 Cambridge St., Cambridge, MA 02139
(617) 496-2481 • fax: (617) 496-2428
e-mail: staff@pluralism.org • Web site: www.fas.harvard.edu

The purpose of Harvard University's Pluralism Project is to help Americans engage with the realities of religious diversity through research, outreach, and the active dissemination of resources. Project leaders authored the book *A New Religious America* and developed the CD-ROM *On Common Ground: World Religions in America*. Articles by project researchers are available on the Pluralism Project's Web site.

**Religious Freedom Coalition (RFC)**
PO Box 77511, Washington, DC 20013
Web site: www.rfcnet.org

The RFC is a conservative Christian coalition that promotes religious freedom and family values-oriented legislation. It advocates the involvement of religious individuals and organizations in politics. The coalition publishes a newsletter and posts news and legislative updates on its Web site.

**Roundtable on Religion & Social Welfare Policy**
Nelson A. Rockefeller Institute of Government
411 State St., Albany, NY 12203
(518) 443-5014 • fax: (518) 443-5705
Web site: www.religionandsocialpolicy.org

The roundtable was created to engage and inform government, religious, and civic leaders about the role of faith-based organizations in America's social welfare system by means of nonpartisan, evidence-based discussions on the potential and pitfalls of such involvement. The organization tracks the George W. Bush administration's use of executive powers and federal agency rule changes, as well as actions by Congress, to advance expanded partnerships between government and faith-based social service providers. It publishes a variety of papers, such as "Is 'Charitable Choice' Compatible with the First Amendment? Is It a Good Idea? Does It Work?"

## Web Site

**Southern Baptist Convention**
Web site: www.sbc.net

The official Web site of the Southern Baptist Convention contains information on the Southern Baptists as well as links to dozens of individual ministry Web sites, many of which voice opinions on family and sanctity-of-life issues.

# Bibliography

## Books

| | |
|---|---|
| Kimberly Blaker | *The Fundamentals of Extremism: The Christian Right in America.* New Boston, MI: New Boston Books, 2003. |
| Edith L. Blumhofer, ed. | *Religion, Politics, and the American Experience: Reflections on Religion and American Public Life.* Tuscaloosa: University of Alabama Press, 2002. |
| E.J. Dionne Jr., Jean Bethke Elshtain, and Kayla M. Drogosz, eds. | *One Electorate Under God?: A Dialogue on Religion and American Politics.* Washington, DC: Brookings Institution Press, 2004. |
| Robert Booth Fowler, Allen D. Hertzke, and Laura R. Olson | *Religion and Politics in America: Faith, Culture, and Strategic Choices.* Boulder, CO: Westview Press, 2004. |
| Esther Kaplan | *With God on Their Side: How Christian Fundamentalists Trampled Science, Policy, and Democracy in George W. Bush's White House.* New York: New Press, 2004. |
| Martin E. Marty with Jonathan Moore | *Politics, Religion, and the Common Good: Advancing a Distinctly American Conversation About Religion's Role in Our Shared Life.* San Francisco: Jossey-Bass, 2000. |
| A. James Reichley | *Faith in Politics.* Washington, DC: Brookings Institution Press, 2002. |
| William Safran, ed. | *The Secular and the Sacred: Nation, Religion, and Politics.* Portland, OR: Frank Cass, 2003. |
| Glenn H. Utter and James L. True | *Conservative Christians and Political Participation: A Reference Handbook.* Santa Barbara, CA: ABC-CLIO, 2004. |
| Jim Wallis | *God's Politics: Why the Right Gets It Wrong and the Left Doesn't Get It.* San Francisco: HarperSanFrancisco, 2005. |
| Stephen H. Webb | *American Providence: A Nation with a Mission.* New York: Continuum, 2004. |
| Richard L. Wood | *Faith in Action: Religion, Race, and Democratic Organizing in America.* Chicago: University of Chicago Press, 2002. |

# Periodicals

Brooke Allen — "Our Godless Constitution: The Faith of Our Founders Definitely Wasn't Christianity," *Nation*, February 21, 2005.

Brian C. Anderson — "Secular Europe, Religious America," *Public Interest*, Spring 2004.

Perry Bacon Jr. — "Trying Out a More Soulful Tone," *Time*, February 7, 2005.

David Batstone and Mark Wexler — "The Right Stuff," *Sojourners*, July 2004.

Steve Bonta — "One Nation Under God," *New American*, July 29, 2002.

Gerard V. Bradley — "Stand and Fight: Don't Take Gay Marriage Lying Down," *National Review*, July 28, 2003.

Patrick J. Buchanan — "Stop Penalizing Religious Politics," *Christian Science Monitor*, March 24, 2005.

Carl M. Cannon — "Bush and God," *National Journal*, January 3, 2004.

Stephen L. Carter — "Liberalism's Religion Problem," *First Things*, March 2002.

E.J. Dionne — "Faith Full—When the Religious Right Was Left," *New Republic*, February 28, 2005.

Gregg Easterbrook — "Religion in America: The New Ecumenicalism," *Brookings Review*, Winter 2002.

Joe Feuerherd — "Re-Igniting the Religious Left," *National Catholic Reporter*, January 23, 2004.

Nancy Gibbs — "Faith in Politics," *Time*, June 21, 2004.

James L. Guth et al. — "Partisan Religion," *Christian Century*, March 21, 2001.

Ted Halstead — "The Chieftains and the Church," *Atlantic Monthly*, January/February 2004.

Doug Ireland — "Republicans Relaunch the Antigay Culture Wars," *Nation*, October 20, 2003.

Richard D. Land — "Why Christians Should Vote Their Values," *National Right to Life News*, October 2000.

Ayelish McGarvey — "Reaching to the Choir," *American Prospect*, April 2004.

Chris W. Mooney — "W.'s Christian Nation: How Bush Promotes Religion and Erodes the Separation of Church and State," *American Prospect*, June 2003.

James Morone — "In God's Name: Past Presidents Have Shown There's a Better Way to Invoke God in Wartime," *American Prospect*, May 2003.

Robert O'Neil — "Church-State Separation: A View from the Pew," *Free Inquiry*, April/May 2004.

John O'Sullivan — "How the Media Miss the Religion Story," *World & I*, September 2004.

*Philadelphia Inquirer* — "Religious Right Seeks Judiciary That Dissolves Church-State Separation," April 30, 2005.

David Plotz — "The Protestant Presidency: Why Jews, Mormons, and Catholics Still Can't Get Elected President," *Slate.com*, February 11, 2000.

Ramesh Ponnoru — "Secularism and Its Discontents: The Debate Over Religion and Politics Is in Desperate Need of Sanity," *National Review*, December 27, 2004.

Eyal Press — "Closing the 'Religion Gap,'" *Nation*, August 30, 2004.

Amy Sullivan — "The Religion Gap: Can Democrats Breach It?" *Commonweal*, September 10, 2004.

Michael Tackett — "Abortion Remains One of the Most Stark Dividing Lines in Politics," *Chicago Tribune*, January 20, 2003.

Karen Tumulty — "Battling the Bishops," *Time*, June 21, 2004.

Karen Tumulty and Matthew Cooper — "What Does Bush Owe the Religious Right?" *Time*, February 7, 2005.

Mara Vanderslice — "Religious Democrats?" *Sojourners*, May 2004.

Jim Wallis — "Dangerous Religion: George W. Bush's Theology of Empire," *Sojourners*, September/October 2003.

Jim Wallis — "The Democrats' Religion Problem," *Sojourners*, February 2004.

Kenneth T. Walsh and Jeff Kaus — "Separate Worlds," *U.S. News & World Report*, October 25, 2004.

Ellen Willis — "Freedom from Religion: What's at Stake in Faith-Based Politics," *Nation*, February 19, 2001.

Claudia Winkler — "Religion, Politics, and the New Obtuseness," *Weekly Standard*, November 29, 2004.

Louise Witt — "Whose Side Is God On?" *American Demographics*, February 1, 2004.

# Index